TRAMPING IN SKYE

By

B. H. HUMBLE

Photo   R. Anderson

SGURR NAN GILLEAN FROM BLAVEN

FOREWORD

MANY of the Skye place-names have alternative spellings; in this book the Ordnance Survey spelling has been given throughout. Where there is controversy as to the meaning of the Gaelic names I have given what seems to be the most appropriate.

I wish to thank Messrs R. Anderson, J. Banford, W. J. MacArthur and the Rev. A. E. Robertson, for permission to reproduce their photographs. Robert Anderson also drew the map of Skye, while Mr Robertson gave some kindly help when the book was in the making. My thanks are also due to Jack Fleming, who designed the jacket.

For allowing me to use an article which appeared originally in *Chambers's Journal* I have to thank the Editor of that magazine.

B. H. H.

COMELY BANK,
   DUMBARTON,
      April 1933.

CONTENTS

CONTENTS

ILLUSTRATIONS

PHOTOGRAPHS

MAPS

" Who has the hills for lover, he finds them wondrous kind."

TRAMPING IN SKYE

CHAPTER I

THE ROAD TO THE ISLES

Where hangs the deep blue vault of heaven,
   Star-powdered, flashing gold.
Where sing our hills the same sweet song,
   The tale is never old.
Where flaming colours speed the sun,
   Where westering shadows glow,
Where everything in nature calls,
   Oh! pack your kit and go.

ANON.

"WE'LL walk round Skye." The Red One, a Highlander, was full of enthusiasm, and managed to convey to me, a mere Lowlander, something of the call of the hills. We travelled by the West Highland route from Queen Street Station, Glasgow. This is one of the few railway journeys in Britain where the tourist has no need of a magazine or a newspaper. Many times now I have travelled by that route: in high summer with blue skies, purpling mountains and sparkling burns; in autumn with the heather in full bloom and the glorious ruddy red tints of the bracken splashing the hillsides; in midwinter with the hills majestic among the snows, and in spring when gully-streaked with old névé. Now that the mountains are old friends the succeeding well-known vistas revealed by the twists and

I

turns of the railway only serve to increase the charm of the journey. There is a forenoon train, but my preference will always be for the early one at 5.45. That was our choice, and the glory of a West Highland morning kept us awake.

Up by the sea-lochs, by Rhu and Garelochhead, with a first glimpse of the hills of Argyll at Whistlefield. At Arrochar old man Cobbler and his satellites —The Brack, Narnain and A'Chrois—greeted us, each with memories of happy week-ends on the hills. Just a glimpse up Glencroe to Beinn an Lochain and a short sight of Ben Vorlich away to the north of Glen Loin before the train cuts through the glen to Loch Lomond. From this viewpoint Ben Lomond, shorn of his broad shoulders so familiar to us in the south, loses much of his impressiveness. Northwards again, and I love that bit at Inveruglas where the hills seem suddenly to come apart, revealing Coiregrogain and the mass of Ben Vane. Now by the flanks of Ben Vorlich across rushing burns, very torrents after rain, to Ardlui and the entrance to the Highlands. Glen Falloch is a fitting gateway to the North, with the Crianlarich giants guarding the east portal and the Tyndrum mountains the west.

Now the climb commences, a climb which terminates at 1500 feet on the wilds of Rannoch Moor. One by one the mountains come into view; first Beinn Chabhair, then An Caisteal and the Twistin Hill; then Cruach Ardrain and, dominating them all, the twin cones of Ben More and Am Binnein. The tramper would fain alight here and spend a day on the ridges, but fine though they are in summer, they are ever so much better among the snows of winter. Just after crossing the River Fillan a last glimpse south gives a fine view of Cruach Ardrain, guarded by those splendid outliers, Grey Height and Stob Garbh. Three miles farther up Strath Fillan there is another mountain vista; of Glen Coninish and Beinn Laoigh, that shapely peak, and his consorts, Ben Oss and Beinn Dubh-craig. The great centre corrie of Laoigh is one of the finest amongst our Scottish mountains, but, like many others, is most impressive in winter-time.

Now northwards by the side of the old road, while across the glen the embankments of the new road still scar the hillside. Rounding Beinn Odhar the glorious sweep of Beinn Dorain comes into view. The train curves round by the viaduct, passing a lonely clump of trees which shelter a house rejoicing in the name of Auch. Then past Bridge of Orchy to Loch Tulla, whose fir-trees and background of the Black Mount and Stob Ghabhar have enticed many a photographer. Here the new highway to Glencoe strikes off to the west. Just where rail and motor road part company there is a brief glimpse of that wild corrie between Beinn an Dòthaidh and Beinn Achaladair.

Beyond Gorton the journey across the peaty wastes of Rannoch Moor can be made only by train. The mountains now seem far away; to the west Clachlet and the hills of Glencoe, with Buchaille Etive Mòr guarding the pass; to the east a glimpse of Ben Alder and the perfect cone of Schiehallion. All around are deadly peat-bogs and little lochans known only to the fisherman, and at Rannoch station the train will be sure to set down oilskin-clad figures with all the impedimenta of the angler's craft.

Then across the north-west stretch of the moor to Corrour siding. To the tramper it will at once conjure up memories of that other Corrour, the bothy at the foot of the Devil's Point in the Larig Ghru. And like the bothy it will become a trampers' rendezvous. For now that there is a Youth Hostel at Loch Ossian, a mile away, Corrour is the trampers' gateway to the Grampians. Even when the chain of hostels is completed none can hope to rival that converted boat-house surrounded on three sides by water and guarded by six fine Munros.

The walker who wishes to see something of these mountains could leave the early train at Corrour, spend some time there, and join the afternoon train. If a member of the Scottish Youth Hostels Association he may spend a night at Corrour, and stretch his legs on Càrn Dearg or Sgòr Gaibhre. Accommodation is limited, and previous arrangement should be made. This hostel is closed during August, September and October. Let the tramper go on to Skye in high summer and return to visit Loch Ossian and the wild mountains around when the snow lies deep.

Due north once more by Loch Treig, where man is fighting nature, then into the Glen of Spean. At Tulloch a motor road again adjoins the railway, and

Photo

B. H. Humble

EARLY MORNING—YOUTHS' HOSTEL—LOCH OSSIAN

[Facing page 4

Photo   ON THE ROAD TO THE ISLES.—THE HARBOUR AT MALLAIG   *R. Anderson*

[Facing page 5

the River Spean, with foaming gorges and deep dark pools, accompanies it for six miles. And so under the shadow of the highest of Scotland's mountains to Fort William. Here the back of the train becomes the front. The wise traveller, who has by this time wangled his way into the restaurant-car, which affords a much better view of the countryside, should remember that some of the trains disconnect this portion at Fort William.

When the train winds round at Corpoch there is, if the gods be kind, a glimpse of Ben Nevis, and his southern shoulder, Càrn Dearg. Usually mist hides the great peak. Westwards now to the isles, by sea-loch and land-loch, through the land of Morar. This is Prince Charlie's own country. From now until the tramper leaves Skye every village will have some memories of that Prince of Adventurers. Charles Edward Stuart and Samuel Johnson are two names writ large across the history of Skye. The tramper will not bother about the stout Englishman, who rode on pony-back, and whom the mountains only " affected with astonishment." But he will pay tribute to the Jacobite whose long arduous journeys across country in the Outer Hebrides, in Skye and on the mainland, make him a fitting Prince of Trampers.

It was into Loch-nan-Uamh his ship came sailing, and he landed, without an army, and attempted to win a crown. It was from Loch-nan-Uamh his ship sailed out a year later, his cause lost and himself a fugitive.

The train winds by Loch Eilside to Glenfinnan, where once he raised his standard, and then by Loch Eilt and Loch Ailort to the golden sands of Arisaig and a first glimpse of the enchanted isles. Only a few miles now, by Morar, and the train reaches its journey's end at Mallaig. Some day I shall have time to explore that village. Up till now I have been so eager to get to Skye that only the road to the ferry or the steamer has concerned me. The chief recollection is the dominating smell of fish and the queer booths at the harbour which serve as shops. The last lap commences, and the ship chugs its way up the Sound of Sleat, past the rocky coastline of Knoydart and Loch Hourn, through the narrows, and so to Kyle of Lochalsh. Only the ferry now separates us from the Isle of Mist.

CHAPTER II

Think of cloud on Beinn na Caillich,
    Jagged Cuillin soaring high,
Scent of peat and all the glamour
    Of the misty Isle of Skye.

A. M. HARBORD.

THE misty isle certainly lived up to its reputation on that first day. Drizzling rain greeted us when we landed at Kyleakin and we saw nothing of the hills; all were enveloped in a misty greyness. Our first object was a visit to Castle Moil, where once a Viking's daughter ruled as Queen. She married a Macdonald, and seems to have learned well from him the gospel of thriftiness, for they say she extorted payment from every ship that passed through Kyleakin (the Strait of Haco). Little of the castle now remains, other than the ancient keep with its twelve-foot-thick walls.

Then we set off on the road to Broadford, and the rain became heavier.

" If you are a delicate man,
    And of wetting your skin are shy,
I'd have you know, before you go,
    You had better not think of Skye."

We soon learned the truth of Sheriff Nicolson's words. Skye rain is very wetting! We believe now

7

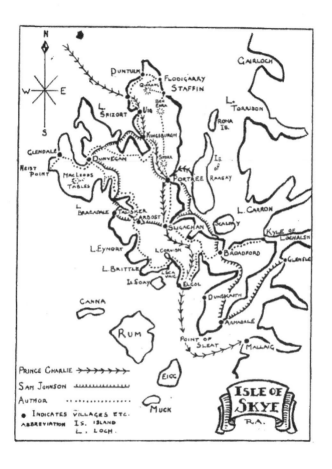

ISLE OF SKYE

R.A.

Prince Charlie →→→→→
Sam Johnson ⊢⊢⊢⊢⊢⊢⊢
Author ···············
● Indicates Villages etc.
Abbreviation   Is. Island
              L. Loch.

that nothing other than a complete set of oilskins, together with thigh-boots, would keep it out. We wore what an enthusiastic salesman had assured us were equally efficient as waterproof ground-sheets or capes. They may have been good ground-sheets—we did not test them—they were woefully inefficient as capes.

The road keeps within sight of the sea for the first few miles, then winds inland at Lusa, where it is joined by the road from Kylerhea. There are no trees and no shelter for miles on end. We plugged on, and soon became thoroughly soaked. Our only consolation was the knowledge that our packs were waterproof and that they contained some dry clothing.

With our packs feeling mighty heavy, and our feet feeling mighty sore, the much-talked-of " charm of Skye " seemed but a myth that first day. At last, isolated cottages appeared, and became more frequent. There are milestones in Skye; never yet have I been able to decipher any figures on them. As each cottage materialized out of the mist we thought ourselves at our journey's end. But Broadford straggles round the bay for three miles, and the cottage we were making for was at the farther end of the village. Soon we were fixed up with a room and a plentiful supply of hot water.

We decided afterwards that, from the walker's point of view, the fact that hot water can be obtained at any cottage at any time is one of the minor charms of Skye. Fuel is abundant, each cottage has its own

peat-stack and the kitchen fire is never allowed to
go out.

As if to make up for its previous absence, the sun
came out and shone gloriously that evening. We
wandered round the village and out to the pier.
Here we were greatly amused to find a bill pub-
lished by the Board of Agriculture and Fisheries
which gravely informed us that it was illegal to
catch lobsters measuring less than six inches from
tip to tail. We at once had a vision of old Broadford
fishermen measuring lobsters with six-inch rules and
swearing in Gaelic.

Never have I seen such rapid sky changes as in
Broadford that night, with the mist rising and
falling, revealing momently the stark black of the
hills behind. Every variety of cloud was present in
the sky. Over in Applecross the hills were shrouded
in dark, lowering clouds; above, the sky was blue
and summery, while Beinn na Caillich, towering
behind us, was wrapped in a black stormy mantle,
as if a thunderstorm were raging on its summit.
Broadford Bay reminded me of the lower reaches
of Loch Lomond, for it seemed like an inland loch,
shut in by Applecross and Scalpay, and, like Loch
Lomond, bore fairy islands—the purple Crowlin
Isles and Pabay—on its bosom.

A little way south of Broadford, nestling under
the shadow of the Beinn, are the ruins of the farm
of Corriechatachan (the Corrie of Wild Cats), where
came Boswell and Johnson a hundred-and-twenty
years ago. A track leads down from the main road

and across the River Broadford, but little of the farm now remains. This was the only house they visited twice, and anyone reading both Johnson's book and Boswell's comments will see that they regarded it as the most hospitable. Johnson relates how " we were very willing to return." And that Skye had given to the English critic something of its kindliness is evidenced by his almost human behaviour on his second visit. Boswell tells how Johnson was " merry to a high degree," and even so far forgot himself as to take a married woman on his knee, the while Boswell himself became very drunk. From here these, the vanguard of the English tourists, went to Raasay. I like Boswell's description of " one of the four stout rowers—a MacLeod—a robust, black-haired fellow, half-naked and bareheaded, something between a Wild Indian and an English Tar."

Then in the gloaming, round a big peat fire, we heard of the legend of the Norse Princess who came with Haco's invaders and lived in Castle Moil, at Kyleakin. But she pined for her homeland, and commanded that, on her death, she should be buried on the bleak summit of Beinn na Caillich, where her bier would be ever swept by the cold north winds of her native land. At a later date, after we had scrambled through the bracken and the heather, toiled up the steep scree and emerged from the cold mist to the shelter of the huge cairn on the top of this mountain, we doubted if her followers, however loyal, could have carried out her wishes. The fact remains that the cairn on the

summit of Beinn na Caillich is by far the largest of
any on the Skye hills, and much bigger than the usual
cairn on the mainland mountains, while the very
name means " Mount of the Old Woman."

Next morning we took the road to Strathaird,
across the island, and straight away passed into the
land of fairies. There are stories innumerable of
fairy dwellings in this valley. Just at the roadside
is the Allt an t-Sithein (Burn of the Fairies), and
near by is a fairies' hillock where the wee folk used
to dance to the pipes in the gloaming. That word
" Sithein " occurs again and again in the map of
Skye; there are Fairies' Burns, Fairies' Caves,
Fairies' Hills, Fairies' Lochs and Fairies' Bridges.
There are still old folks in the island who believe
in fairies, and surely more than mere legend and
imagination is responsible for these names. Even
such an august body as the British Association has
debated this problem. At their annual meeting
in 1932 Canon MacCulloch, who knows the Isle of
Mist so well, invited them to consider if the Skye
fairies were not actually a race of prehistoric people
of small stature.

Maybe they were, and it is legend and imagination that has clothed them in green, made them
emerge on dark nights and work good or ill down
through the centuries.

It was a pleasant walk through Strath Suardal,
round Beinn na Caillich, Beinn Dearg Mhòr and
Beinn Dearg Bheag, the three mountains comprising
the Red Hills. Only afterwards did we appreciate

the significance of the name. The rocks and stones of these hills and of the Red Cuillin are of a much lighter colour than the gabbro rock of the Black Cuillin. In sunshine, and especially in the evening, their summits take on a reddish glow.

Soon we came to the little loch of Cill Chriosd, where the water-lilies were in bud. The centuries flew back once more. In Skye, with the map and some knowledge of the meaning of the place-names, one can learn much of the history and folklore of the island; for most of the places have stories attached to them, whether of the fairies, of the Fingalian warriors, of the first Christians, of the Norse invaders or of the Celts, right down to Prince Charlie's time. Cill Chriosd means "the Church of Christ." Cill or Kil occurs frequently in Skye names, the original meaning being a monk's cell, or holy place, indicating where Columba's missionaries first preached the Faith. Near by are the ruins of the church from which the loch gets its name.

Now a leap forward of hundreds of years. Just farther on are the disused marble-works. Marble of good quality was quarried there last century, and they say that part of the high-altar of Iona Cathedral is made of Strath marble. Now, like the church, only ruins remain.

We walked on, and then:

> " At a clear open turn in the roadway,
>   My passion went up with a cry,
> For the wonderful mountain of Blaven
>   Was heaving his huge bulk on high."

So sang Alexander Smith, and no lines could be more appropriate. Never before had we seen anything like that shattered mass of wild black crags which so suddenly came into view. Standing alone, apart from the Cuillin, Blaven is indeed a monarch among mountains, and more than Smith have claimed it as the grandest mountain in all Scotland. Different authorities have given Blaven such meanings as " The Mountain of Bloom," " The Blowy Mount " or " The Warm Mount," but I like best the story of the Skye man who was asked about it and said: " Oh, it will just be meaning a grand mountain."

It held our gaze as we continued to Loch Slapin. Hereabouts, on the south side of the road, are the remains of what was once a stone circle of the Druids, and maybe in their pagan rites Blaven was one of their worshipped gods. The Ordnance Map shows many of these stone circles in Skye. Little remains of them now, so that their exact sites are difficult to find. Passing the little village of Torran we reached the loch-side, where we lunched, and watched great banks of mist sweep down to hide Blaven's summit from view.

On the hillside near by were a herd of beautiful ponies. White, brown, black and dappled, and all with long fair manes, they might have come straight out of a circus. These ponies are hired to wanderers bound for Coruisk, or fishermen going to Camasunary, and to other poor mortals who cannot enjoy shank's nag.

We crossed the island again through Strath Mòr. Bleak and desolate, this must be one of the loneliest glens in Skye. It has an eerie reputation, too, for they say Loch na Sguabaidh is haunted, and that no young girl will go near it after dusk, lest she be seized by the water-horse which dwells therein and feeds on beautiful maidens!

For three-and-a-half miles we saw nor man nor tree nor dwelling. Purple Blaven towered behind us. The Red Hills shut us in on either side. We were treading on hallowed ground, for we were retracing the footsteps of Prince Charlie. It was through this glen the wanderer fled on his way from Portree to Elgol. We can well imagine how, among the awful desolation, he turned to his guide and said: " I'm sure the Devil could not find me now."

> " To see our bonny Prince again,
>   So gallant, brave and fair,
> The clean wind rushing down the glen
>   Stirring his shining hair."

It was here that we first conceived a great admiration for his walking powers. Portree to Elgol by the road is about thirty miles. The Prince, and MacLeod his guide, did the whole distance without ever going near a road, and climbed over Beinn Dearg on the way. A modern tramper would find that journey testing his powers.

The hills were disgorging themselves of the previous week's rain. Every burn was a foaming torrent and all the little lochs stretching through the glen had overflowed their banks. The path had a disconcerting habit of disappearing into lochs every now and then, so that we were constantly wading through water and marshes. As we came down the valley to Loch Ainort, first the pyramidal Glamaig, then the ridge of Beinn Dearg, and finally the curiously shaped Marsco came into view, and for the rest of the day these were our companions.

At the crofting township of Luib we sought milk, and were offered tea. We should have thought milk easier to obtain, but were soon to know that the Skye man's passion is for tea. And is there any tea like Skye tea?—black, strong and boiled, and mightily refreshing! MacCulloch states that the orgy of tea-drinking, which has replaced much of the whisky-drinking of earlier days, "is now one of the most fruitful sources of ill-health in Skye." Between us, we burned our palates with gallons of that tea, and survived.

From Loch Ainort a splendid new road goes round the coast by Moll to Loch Sligachan, but we preferred the old one over Druim nan Cleochd, well named the Stony Ridge. This road, which has been untouched since the new one was constructed, is full of pot-holes and looks as if it had been under shell-fire. It must have been a terror to the motorist; now, like other old roads in Skye, it is left in splendid isolation to the tramper, and gives a much better walk than by following the coastline.

It climbs high, curves round Glamaig, and drops down to Loch Sligachan at Sconser Lodge. This countryside is known as "Lord Macdonald's Deer Forest." Like many of the deer forests on the mainland it is now bare of trees, and does not carry many deer. Once Skye was overrun with deer. Ossian has many stories of those mighty warriors Cuchullain and Fingal and their deer-hunts in Skye: in one of them he tells of 6000 deer being slain by 3000 hounds in Strath Mòr.

As we came over the hill the island of Raasay came into view, and we could make out the pier and the remains of the iron-works. This is another of the Skye industries which have fallen by the way, though recently there has been talk of its being revived.

An outbreak of barking and bleating greeted our ears, and on climbing a dyke by the roadside we discovered, in a deep-walled pen, four men, four dogs and half-a-hundred sheep. There were no modern methods of sheep-shearing: the poor beast was up-ended and its whole shaggy coat clipped off in one piece with huge scissors. The skill and quickness were remarkable, for, though the sheep were struggling all the time, skin after skin was clipped off without mishap.

Soon we arrived at the village of Sconser, where once the history of Britain—maybe of the world—was altered. In the plotting previous to the '45 Rebellion the chiefs of Skye had promised their support to the Jacobite cause. When the Prince arrived in the West Highlands without a French army they refused to "come out" with their clans.

Charlie won the heart and allegiance of the chief of the Clanranald branch of the Macdonalds, and sent the young Clanranald to Skye in a last effort to persuade the great chiefs to rally to his aid.

The MacLeod and The Macdonald met the Prince's emissary at Sconser. Though Clanranald pled the Prince's cause with youthful eloquence they still refused their help. Some have it that, had the Prince gone on from Derby, with his small army, he would have won through. Perhaps he would. Had The MacLeod and The Macdonald given their full support it is certain he would have won through. For then the Highlands would have been absolutely solid behind Charlie; the Lowlands would have joined in, and nothing could have stopped him.

And then? No Napoleonic Wars? America still a British colony?—for there would have been no George the Third to bungle matters. No Great War? These are some of the might-have-beens had that conference at Sconser had a different outcome.

We were very fortunate in obtaining a night's lodging at Sconser, where there are only a few cottages, and in the holiday season there is seldom accommodation for the casual walker. Again there was instant hot water. After a good tea and letter-writing we wandered through the village. It is so overshadowed by the mass of Glamaig that they say the sun seldom shines in Sconser.

The wee post-office down by the loch-side amused us; later, in the smaller villages, we saw many queer cottages where His Majesty's Service is carried on.

The Red One suggested it would be a good idea to collect photographs of all the post-offices in Skye, while I maintained that photographs of the amazing assortment of wares in the windows of the " General Merchants " would make a more amusing collection. Sconser, though small, boasts a " boot and shoe repairer." That cottage calls aloud for a photograph.

Later that evening we had the good fortune to fall in with John Mackenzie. We had heard of him, for his name appears in all books on Skye, and his fame has even been sung in verse:

> " Sing the praise of doughty John,
>   Lord of crag and boulder,
> Peak and gully, slab and scree,
>   Pinnacle and shoulder;
> Sure of foot and keen of eye,
>   Cheery words to hail us;
> Ready still with rope and hand
>   When the footholds fail us."

D. F. R.

He is the most famous mountain guide in Britain: a man among men, white-bearded, ruddy complexioned and clear of eye, and though over seventy he was, up till a few years ago, leading the way to the mountain-tops. He does not climb now, but is still a mighty fisherman. What a grand life Mackenzie has had! He has watched the growth of rock-climbing in Skye from its infancy, and was with the parties when many of the peaks were first climbed. He was one of the first to climb the " inaccessible pinnacle " of Sgurr Dearg, and it is fitting indeed that Sgurr Mhic Coinnich should perpetuate his memory. Away back about 1890 he was climbing with the pioneers of the Scottish Mountaineering Club, and since then with hundreds of cragsmen who have followed in their footsteps. His love for the Cuillin is unbounded. He counts them as his children, and has stories of every peak and pinnacle, every corrie and lochan. When he heard that we wanted to do a climb when thoroughly fit he said that Sgurr Alaisdair, the highest Cuillin, was "just a walk" from Glen Brittle.

(For alternative routes see page 91.)

Photo   *J. Banford*

JOHN MACKENZIE OF SCONSER GIVES SOME ADVICE

[Facing page 20

Photo

A HEBRIDEAN SUNSET

A. E. Robertson

[Facing page 21

CHAPTER III

SLIGACHAN AND PORTREE

O for the Hills of Skye!
With storm-wracked cliffs on high,
Where sunset's streaming fire
Drapes Sgurr nan Gillean's spire;
Where climbers gladly greet
Rock safe for hands and feet,
On which dear life to trust
However fierce the gust.
O for the hills of Skye!
Dark Cuillin Hills of Skye.

L. PILKINGTON, *The Hills of Peace.*

NEXT day we contented ourselves with an easy trek, eleven miles to Portree. The mist hung low for the first two days, so that we had no far-off glimpse of the Black Cuillin, the wildest rock-crags in all Britain. We had heard of them: we had seen photographs of them: no story or photograph could do justice to a first sight at close quarters of these huge crags of black rock. At Sligachan Bridge we were almost surrounded by mountains—the Red Cuillin to the east, Ben Lee to the north and the Black Cuillin to the south. Mist still hung about the summit of Sgurr nan Gillean, then gradually lifted, and we could pick out his four pinnacles one behind the other. To those who know only the smoother hills of the mainland it seems impossible that these mountains could be ascended, yet all have been climbed in hundreds of ways.

Sligachan is the mountaineering centre for Skye. There is no village. The inn is the only building, and is rather expensive for the average walker. It is usually fully booked up all summer, so that the tramper who has not made arrangements in advance cannot be sure of obtaining accommodation. He may count himself lucky to get a room at the height of the season and could well spend a day or two there.

If one arrives at noon the place seems deserted. No one remains indoors at Sligachan. Towards evening the different parties will come straggling back: cheery cragsmen after a day testing their powers in the gullies and on the ridges; trampers who have kept to the glens and lesser hills; an artist maybe, who has failed—as many others have failed before him—to put Coruisk on to canvas; and fishermen, with or without their trout or salmon. But all have mighty appetites!

The very building seems to have absorbed something of the spirit of the hills. It contains a wonderful collection of mountain photographs. If these photographs could speak, what stories they would tell! For many of them were taken in the pioneer days, when very heavy and bulky apparatus had to be taken to the mountain tops. The S.M.C. map of the Cuillin, three inches to the mile, is well worth careful study by the tramper. Then there is the "Climbers' Book," with its stories of the earlier climbs, and the "Anglers' Book," with its stories of the fish that were hooked—and the fish that got away.

Some time maybe there will be a Youth Hostel at Sligachan. It is the most central place on the island. Roads radiate east to Broadford, north to Portree and west to Dunvegan, while rough paths lead south-west over Bealach a' Mhaim to Loch Brittle and south-east through Glen Sligachan to Coruisk. We decided to harden our feet on the easier roads of the north part of the island before returning to the rougher journeys among the mountains.

We climbed up by the Allt Dubh and into Glen Varragill. Such was the attraction of the Cuillin that we did much of the road backwards, turning round again and again for yet another glimpse of the mountains. The aspect was ever changing, new peaks came into view, and for a brief time we had a glimpse of the pinnacle ridge of Sgurr nan Gillean.

It was about here that a motorist, taking pity on us with our enormous packs, offered to carry them to Portree. We, like good Scotsmen, refused to part with our belongings. We lunched by a wee burn near the top of the moor. Delicious cold trout, caught by John Mackenzie the previous day, was a fitting dish to eat among the heather.

So refreshed we made good progress down Glen Varragill, and had our first sight of the Trotternish Hills, the Storr and the Old Man. At the lodge we fell in with the keeper, who showed us round his kennels. He was breeding Skye terriers, and had some a week old, just like water-rats. On both sides of his hut were nailed up claws, antlers, skeletons and skulls of birds and beasts with which he waged war, the whole making rather a grisly show.

At two o'clock on the afternoon of " Fair " Saturday we walked through the outsize in squares which is the centre of Portree. It was almost deserted. The street beyond, with the best collection of shops in Skye, kept us a while. There we were able to obtain postcard - photographs of the Cuillin, many of them reproductions of the originals which hang in Sligachan Inn. The chief memory of that street is of a wee shop where we had tea, and consumed a pile of scones fresh from the girdle, and of the blush of the lass behind the counter when we told her she baked the best scones in Skye. There are other delightful shops down by the harbour, where almost anything on earth may be bought.

Portree is the island's capital, but for all that is just a village where life goes leisurely. The normal population is about a thousand. During the summer months this number may be doubled, and with the coming and going of buses, of which there is a good service to all parts of the island, the village has a brisker appearance, only to sink back to its old leisurely ways in the autumn. There is a nine-hole golf course behind the town, but the cinema and the talkies have not yet come to Skye. We hope they never will. Yet Portree is not altogether out of touch with progress. Flying-boats are common in the Hebrides nowadays—the bay is sometimes their base —and there are islesmen who have been up in an aeroplane but have never seen a train.

Even in summer the village does not wake up till the arrival of the mail steamer in the evening. Tourists travelling via Armadale arrive earlier, to be sure, but most of them yet—and wisely—prefer to sail by Broadford and the Sound of Raasay.

We had some time to spare before her arrival, so hired a boat and rowed out to the bay. A splendid harbour it is, guarded by the bold headlands of Creag Mhòr and Ben Tianavaig. The latter name told us it was not always calm, as it means " The Hill of the Stormy Bay." Like other rocky headlands of Skye, the cliffs at the water's edge are riddled with caves. On the north side there is one, called MacCoiter's Cave, which, legend has it, goes right through the island to Loch Bracadale. It was also, at one time, a smugglers' haunt. Farther up the coast the map shows a " Prince Charlie's Cave "; one of the many in the West Highlands which he never visited. If the Prince had lived for a night or two in each of the caves named after him he would never have returned to France after the Rebellion; he would have spent the rest of his life in caves!

When we saw the ship nosing her way into the bay we hurried ashore, to find what appeared to be the whole population of the district gathered at the pier to meet her.

The *Fusilier* now carries on the service. Though she was slow and uncomfortable, many will regret the passing of the good old *Glencoe*. Built in 1846, she had a longer record of service than any steamship in Britain. She lived her life among the West

Highlands, and was known at every harbour and township. For a quarter of a century, up till 1930, she sailed between Mallaig, Kyle, Broadford, Raasay and Portree. She watched over the growth of the tourist traffic to the isles. When she started, motors were unknown, the Cuillin were deemed inaccessible; she lived to see buses await her arrival at every port, and Sligachan acknowledged as the premier centre for rock-climbing in Britain. No longer will we smile at that notice in her third-class cabin:

THIS CABIN HAS ACCOMMODATION
FOR 90 THIRD-CLASS PASSENGERS,
WHEN NOT OCCUPIED BY SHEEP, CATTLE,
CARGO OR OTHER ENCUMBRANCES.

Good old *Glencoe*! MacBrayne must some time write her history.

The ship, that day, carried her heaviest complement of the year, holidaymakers and islanders returning home for the " Fair." It was fine to see the eyes of the exile light up with the Gaelic greeting and the hearty handclasp. Soon the streets were full of laughter and life. A warship was in the bay, and her crew came ashore to swell the throng; after disembarking, the sailors made a bee-line first to the post-office, to send off the inevitable postcards, and then to the bars, to slake their mighty thirst. That over, most of them were on the lookout for something charming with which to while away the evening, and it was surprising how easily they discovered all the secluded nooks around the village.

The pier-dues are amusing. One man is worth four pigs! The notice reads: "Each Pig ½d. Each Person 1d." Just recently man's greater worth has been discovered, the "1d." scored out and "2d." substituted.

The legend of the huge boulder at the water-side, which, they say, a Raasay man threw at his wife, interested me, comparing as it does with our own moors, for are not Dumbuck and Dumbarton Rock stones which fell from the hands of the giant Kilpatrick as he stood on the Long Crags and peppered his brother on the Giant's Causeway?

Portree, too, has its stories of fairies. These were good fairies. They lived on the north side of the bay, and kept cows. They wanted to improve the breed, so they enticed the cows that dwell in the sea to come ashore. The fairies then built a wall of earth between the cows and the sea—and for this purpose earth from a churchyard had to be used—and so prevented them from returning to the water, thus forcing them to stay ashore and mate with the land cows!

On the Sunday afternoon we climbed Beinn na Greine (Mount of the Sun, 1367), that ridge-like hill behind the town. Its northern shoulder is called Fingal's Seat; the Fingal, of course, being the legendary Celtic King of the Isles of the West. Here, they say, he sat and watched his followers with their great hounds chase the deer on the plain below. It is an easy climb, and is said to be a good viewpoint, but the mist hung low and we saw nothing of the Cuillin or the Red Hills. It was a picture only of lowlands and seas. We could follow the waters of Loch Bracadale and Loch Snizort, as they wound their way inland, enclosing between them the whole peninsula of Vaternish. To the north the Storr was hidden, but the Old Man reared his needle-head into the mist and watched over Loch Fada, shining like a gem below him.

It was our intention to spend that night reading on Fancy Hill. The midges had other plans! Though our faces were anointed with anti-midge lotion the brutes drank it, thrived on it, and turned on us, till we came to the conclusion that the father and mother of all midges must live in Portree.

On that first visit we can hardly recall a dull evening, and this one was no exception. The sky cleared, the mist lifted and in a heavenly sunset the very hills were tinged with glory.

Early on the Monday morning we left Portree— Portree of the proud memories. . . .

Here came Ossian's heroes, Cuchullain and Fingal. Perhaps from here Cuchullain, like the brave sons of Skye in later years, set off for the wars. Ossian makes him say: " Retire, for it is night, my love, and the dark wind sighs in thy hair. Retire to the halls of my feasts, and think of the times that are past, for I shall return not till the storm of war is past." Often brave Fingal sat with his followers on that hill we climbed. Tradition and legend are confused, but we like to think that, in those heroic days, the Ossianic heroes really lived and loved in Skye.

Columba, that hardy missionary, undoubtedly knew Portree, for is there not an island in the bay bearing his name and showing ruins of a church built probably by the saint himself? He must have travelled far and wide when he brought Christianity to the then pagan isle. Churches, islands and lochs are dedicated to his memory. He certainly is no legendary figure. Brave, loving and sincere, he and his monks drove out heathen rites and barbarous customs, and set up churches and monasteries, beacons of Christianity.

Came later to Skye the fiery Norsemen, to raid and plunder and burn. Many a time must Portree Bay have sheltered their galleys from the storm. For hundreds of years they dominated the Celt, ruled the island, and gave to it the many Scandinavian place-names which still survive.

Came then a mighty Celt, Somerled, son of the Lord of Argyll, who defeated the Norsemen and drove them from the island. This warrior thus became first Lord of the Isles.

Only once again was the island in danger. Haco gathered a great fleet, sailed to the Outer Hebrides, and proudly led his galleys to Skye, past Portree, and by the Sound of Raasay to Kyleakin. Sailing slowly southwards, his raiders left fire and slaughter in their wake, till at Largs a battle was fought, one autumn day, which ended all. The defeated

Norsemen sought refuge on their ships, but a great storm drove them northwards, to be wrecked on the islands they had once ruled. So ended the Norse power. Haco escaped—to find death at Kirkwall.

Long years passed, with the Celt ever at war with the Scot, till they gave submission to a Stuart king. James the Fifth, with a mighty fleet, entered Portree Bay, then unnamed, but thence known as Port-an-Righ. With stately magnificence he held Court, and his glittering retinue and large army so impressed the island chieftains that they bowed the knee and promised to the House of Stuart loyal allegiance.

That vow the islesmen kept, and Portree's proudest memory is of another Stuart, no ruling King, but an outlaw with a price on his head. Prince Charlie came to Portree, and at the inn sought shelter. The villagers knew well of his presence; knew, too, that there was for his betrayal a reward of £30,000, but there was no hint of treachery. Proud Portree!

(For alternative routes see page 98.)

CHAPTER IV

THE HIGH-LEVEL ROUTE TO STAFFIN

Oh, wildly as the bright day gleamed I climbed the mountain's
    breast,
And when I to my home returned the sun was in the west;
'Twas health and strength, 'twas life and joy, to wander
    freely there,
To drink at the fresh mountain stream, to breathe the
    mountain air.
          DUNCAN BAN McINTYRE, *Last Adieu to the Hills.*

SHERIFF NICOLSON was our guide, for has he not
written: " To climb the Storr and continue along
the ridge to the Quiraing is one of the grandest
promenades in Skye "?   And the words: " He who
would do so must have a long summer day before
him, be strong of foot and light-hearted," rang as a
challenge we could not refuse.

The Cuillin were clear to their tops—a good omen
—at half-past eight, and the sun was shining strongly,
with all the signs of a perfect day to come.   We took
to the moor about two miles north of Portree and
climbed Beinn Mheadhonach on to the main ridge.
A short walk to Beinn a' Chearcaill (1812), a slight
drop to Bealach Mòr (1087), then commenced
a steady plug uphill.   The sun was shining with
tropical heat, and our twenty-pound packs made
it a weary climb from here to the top of the Storr
(2360), but we were amply rewarded.

Lying on the smooth, sheep-cropped turf near the

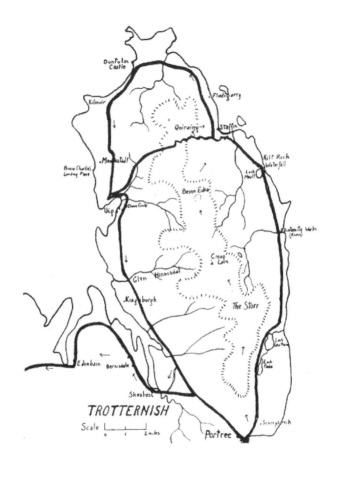

Dunvulm
Castle

Kilmuir

Quiraing →

Flodigarry

Staffin

Kilt Rock
Waterfall

Monkstadt

Prince Charlie's
Landing Place

Loch Mealt

Beinn Edra

Uig

Stone Circle

Dolomite Works
(Ruins)

Craig
a Lain

Glen Hinnisdal

The Storr

Kingsburgh

Loch
Leathan

Loch
Fada

Edinbain

Bernisdale

Skeabost

Scorrybreck

TROTTERNISH

Scale

0   1   2 miles

Portree

cairn we had around us a panorama of the whole north-west, with the sea, island-studded, as dazzlingly blue as any tropical lagoon. Northwards was the ridge of hills, our route, stretching up to the Quiraing and Trotternish Point. Westwards was the peaty moorland, cut up by the crystal-clear sea-lochs, Snizort and Bracadale, and beyond the whole mighty backbone of the Outer Hebrides from Lewis to Barra. Eastwards, below us, the trout lochs, Leatham and Fada, sparkled in the sun, while the islands of Raasay and Rona separated us from the hills of Applecross, showing hundreds of peaks.

We could follow the mainland northwards, Loch Carron, Loch Torridon and Gairloch, while away in the far distance was a hazy promontory we took to be Cape Wrath. Southwards the majestic range of the Black Cuillin compelled the eye. Wild, splintered and jagged, fittingly are they termed the grandest mountains between Switzerland and Norway. The ruddy tops of the Red Hills, gleaming in the sun, showed up the more the black rock of the Cuillin.

The meaning of " The Storr " is " The Steep High Cliff." There are great precipices on its eastern face, and at their foot a weird and fantastic maze of rocks, dominated by a crazy pinnacle, 150 feet high, so well known as " The Old Man of Storr." This cannot be seen from the top, but may be easily visited from the road just to the north of Loch Leatham. The memory of those glorious hours on the summit of the Storr is as a dream. For two hours we lay there, stripped to the waist, and absorbed the health-giving rays of a scorching sun. We were well above the midges and their clan. We were beyond all sight of habitation. We were alone on a mountain-top.

Then onwards, ever northwards, down into the valleys and up again to the hill-tops—on and on— till in the evening we reached Beinn Edra. The weather gods were kind to us and gave us one of those heavenly days when Paradise comes to the Hebrides. It was as a walk along the top of the world, with glorious vistas of seas, islands and mountains.

These hills are entirely different from the Cuillin. The latter are of naked rock, with little vegetation above 2000 feet. The neighbouring peaks are connected together by narrow ridges and, here and there, split up by wild and deep corries. The Trotternish hills are gentle and verdant by comparison. Though there are rocks and precipices along the eastern face, westwards the slopes roll away gradually, and the tops are covered with heather, grass and peat. Their summits are nearly 2000 feet high, while the connecting bealachs are at a height of about 1200 feet.

From the Storr we went down to the watershed, where rise the Lealt river, flowing to the north, and the Lòn Mòr, flowing to the south; then by Bealach Hartaval and along Baca Ruadh (the Red Ridge, 2091), where again we lay on the summit, while our shirts, sweat-soaked, dried in the sun. From there we looked right down the Lealt Valley, but could see nothing of the diatomite-works or the light railway from there to the sea. Like that other Skye venture, the marble-works at Loch Cill Chriosd, it was not fated to survive long.

Our route now lay over Sgurr a' Mhadaidh Ruaidh (the Red Fox's Peak), with a lonely little lochan nestling below it; then we topped in succession Creag à Lain (the Sword Rock, 1993), Beinn Mheadhonach (the Middle Mount, 1895) and finally Beinn Edra (2003). The distance from Portree to Beinn Edra in direct line is about fourteen miles; we calculated we had covered about twenty miles, and the Red One averred that one mile on these hills was equal to two on a road. Such a journey could be performed only on a good day. The ridges are not so definite as those of the Cuillin; in mist one might stray too near the eastern precipices, or down into the western corries, miles from anywhere.

We descended the eastern face of Beinn Edra, and had a two-mile walk through the peat-bogs to the hamlet of Maligar, where, in the bad old days, excisemen, more than once, discovered illicit stills. This consists of only a few thatched shielings planted down on the marshes, with no road near them. We should have kept on the ridge till reaching the road at the Quiraing. Travelling through the peat-hags and marshes was much harder work than tramping the heather on the hill-tops. From leaving the road at nine in the morning till reaching Maligar, at eight at night, we saw no one. Only the scurrying rabbits, the leaping hares and the screeching gulls shared our ramble.

Another two miles took us to Staffin. The long trek left us both very weary, and we were in despair when two houses refused us lodging. But about nine o'clock, at a wee farm, we were made welcome, and regaled like the Prodigal Son. Our feet were in a sorry mess, and I laugh when I remember how, in the dusk, we sat in the farmyard with our feet immersed in tubs of hot water and the whole household listening to our tale. The supper—a hearty Skye supper—and we were as giants refreshed.

We slept soundly that night—at least I did—for when I woke up at 11 A.M. the Red One was returning from a bathe. When he said, " This is a grand place, we'll stay here for another day," I heartily agreed. For it is one of the charms of a walking tour that there need be no fixed itinerary. A hearty welcome, a comfortable bed and good feeding often upset all plans.

All visitors have their favourite among the many delightful villages in Skye. To us, that green afternoon, Staffin was a very Paradise. Unfortunately there is not much accommodation for casual walkers, but those who carry tents would find it an ideal camping site. A week could well be spent at Staffin: there is grand bathing; the Mealt Waterfall and the Kilt Rock to visit; Beinn Edra to climb and the Quiraing to explore.

The afternoon we spent sea-bathing and sun-bathing. In the early evening we walked along the Portree road to Loch Mealt, from where we had a good view of the Kilt Rock before returning along

Photo   *W. J. MacArthur*

LOOKING OUT FROM THE QUIRAING

[Facing page 37

MEALT WATERFALL AND KILT ROCK

the top of the cliffs as far as Staffin House. A company of Marines were stationed here during the troublous times fifty years ago when Skye men protested vigorously against hundreds of crofters being evicted from their dwellings to make way for sheep-farms. Happily, since then, governments have been more sympathetic, and now encourage and help the crofters. The clan chiefs have played their part and, since the War, have sold thousands of acres to create small-holdings.

This was the hottest day of our fortnight. In the evening the air became close and heavy: about midnight a terrific thunderstorm awakened us. We had never seen anything like that display of lightning. At first there were only mild forked flashes, but later forks blazed away in all parts of the sky, and several times balls of blazing light appeared, with zigzag flashes radiating from them. These were so vivid as to be almost blinding—one moment pitch-darkness, the next the rocks of the Quiraing as clear as in daylight.

In the morning we expected to find the burn in spate and the Scouts' tent beside it washed into the sea. Rain must have fallen somewhere, but not at Staffin, though there was still a heaviness and dullness in the air.

"Friendly atmospheres, kindly people, have a way of leaving something of their friendliness and kindliness behind them." At Staffin we met with overwhelming kindness, and were reluctant to leave.

(For alternative routes see page 103.)

CHAPTER V

THE QUIRAING, DUNTULM, UIG AND EDINBAIN

Lands may be fair ayont the sea,
Yet Hieland hills and glens for me!

IT was dull and windy, a fitting day to visit such a place as the Quiraing. It is difficult to describe this weird place, for it is a freak of nature, such as the Whangie of the Stockiemuir Road, but a hundred times more awesome. We left the road about two miles out of Staffin and climbed to the foot of the cliffs. The path leads by the Needle Rock to the grand amphitheatre. It can be entered through other corries, though this is the easiest route. Afterwards we were greatly amused on reading an old book about Skye to find the climb to the Quiraing described as " critical and dangerous," and to read how a man of the party " began to show signs of losing his head; he was giddy and nervous, evidently quite unable either to proceed or retrace his steps." Those were the days when the Cuillin were a sacred mystery; now the Quiraing is the haunt of every tourist, and hundreds climb the high Cuillin.

The path is fairly steep, but could not be called difficult, though there are a great number of loose stones, especially when passing the Needle Rock. This weird pinnacle, a brother to the Old Man of Storr, is about ninety feet high, and unclimbable.

Passing it on our right we entered the vast amphitheatre of rocks with the " table " in the centre.
This is the most curious feature, for one would not
expect to find a huge, flat slab of rock, 100 ft. by
60 ft., covered with grass, amid such desolation.
On the inland side rise the rocky crags of Meall na
Suiramach (the Hill of the Water Nymph) and all
around are fantastic pillars and pinnacles.   From
the " table " we had a grand view seaward through
the corries, with the lochs Hasco and Fada in the
foreground, and Flodigarry and the blue Atlantic
beyond, the bright greens and blues contrasting
strangely with the naked black rocks around.

They say that, in olden days, the Quiraing was
a sanctuary for sheep.   Even on that summer day
the whole place was gloomy and awe-inspiring.   In
winter, with the wind howling and the rain lashing,
the Quiraing must be the very haunt of the Devil.

Some translate Quiraing as " The Pit of Rock
Pillars "; others have it that it means " The Pit of
the Men of Fingal."   One can well imagine that
Ossian's warrior giants would make this wild place
their haunt in the far-off days.

Returning to the road we set off northwards.   This
is a pleasant hilly road, with unexpected little lochans
here and there.   Soon we came to Flodigarry House,
splendidly situated among trees, and facing to the
south.   It will always be remembered as Flora Macdonald's first home after her marriage.   Just recently
the house was converted into an hotel, so that here,
as in the Royal Hotel at Portree, where once Prince

Charlie slept, any traveller can live and dream through the romantic past.

Beyond Flodigarry the road turns inland through the scattered village of Kilmaluag to the west coast of the island. From our first glimpse of the ruins very little seemed to remain of the ancient castle of Duntulm, but when we stood on the exposed headland we could see the full extent of the foundations.

For hundreds of years this was the seat of the Lords of the Isles, and here they ruled as kings. It is the best situated of all the Skye castles, and it is a great pity it is not still the Macdonalds' stronghold, as Dunvegan Castle is the MacLeods'. Probably before the time of the Macdonalds it was a fort of the Vikings and of the early Celts. It was used up to the beginning of the eighteenth century and then suddenly left empty. Exposed, as it is, to the full blast of the Atlantic, its thick walls crumbled rapidly. No one seems to know exactly why the castle was abandoned. There are stories of a nursemaid who dropped a child out of a window and so brought bad luck on the family, and of its being haunted by the ghost of Donald Gorme, one of the earlier chiefs. Grooves on the rocks in front of the castle are pointed out as the marks made by the keels of galleys when they were drawn ashore.

Near by is the "Hill of Pleas," where the chiefs dispensed rude justice. No jury was necessary in those days. The accused was put inside a barrel liberally studded with nails and then rolled down the hill. This served both as a trial and a verdict. If the poor wretch survived he was " Not Guilty," if he didn't he was " Guilty." There is another grim story of how, when the first gallows was erected, they immediately hanged an old (and innocent) man just to see how it worked.

The Trotternish district has many associations with the Norse occupation of Skye, and it is probable that the Vikings also used this " Hill of Pleas." An analogy can be found in the " Law Mount," on the Parliament Plain of Thingvellir, in Iceland, from where the early Viking settlers to that country proclaimed their laws.

The rain came on, the wind rose, and on the headland we were almost blown off our feet. We continued southwards by Score Bay. For nearly a mile the road keeps close to the sea, and we were exposed to the full blast of a south-west wind. Rhu Bornaskitaig, the point to the south of Score Bay, is the traditional spot where the Macdonalds first reached Skye. Two galleys were racing for land, the first man ashore to own the island. Prow to prow they came, leaping over the waves. Then up stood Donald, son of Reginald MacSomerled, cut off his own hand and threw it ashore on the rocks, so that the flesh and blood of a Macdonald first touched Skye.

About two miles south we left the road to visit the ancient burial-place of the Macdonalds of the Isles and pay homage at the grave-side of Flora, the best remembered of them all. They say that the huge

Iona Cross of white stone which marks her grave in Kilmuir can be seen far out at sea.

The road now leads inland through fertile land and cultivated fields, which contrasted strangely with the desolate moorlands on the east between Sligachan and Portree. There were frequent cottages the whole way to Uig. Between the road and the sea once lay Loch Chaluim Chille. On an island in the loch was situated, as the name implies, a monastery of St Columba. After repeated attempts the loch was drained, about a hundred years ago. During these operations prehistoric canoes were found, which were assumed to have been used as ferries between the island and the shore. It is more than a mile from the road to the site of the monastery, of which very little remains. Nearer the sea is higher ground, surmounted by Càrn Liath, an ancient burial-ground.

Farther south a cart track leads down to Monkstadt, and beyond the house is Prince Charlie's Point, where he first set foot on the island. Travelling on we soon came to the hill road from Staffin, and Uig lay before us. Where the road winds down by a hairpin bend we left it and followed a path to the lower road. Uig surprised us. We did not expect to find such a big village in the northern part of the island. It has actually garages, buses and tearooms.

With the opening of the Youth Hostel, trampers will soon get to know Uig better. Though it is far from the Cuillin there is much of interest in the surrounding country. Kilmuir, Duntulm and the

Quiraing are within easy distance; Glen Uig can be explored and Beinn Edra climbed.

Again we found suitable lodgings, and proved what good trenchermen we were. That quiet night at Uig is a happy memory. I had strained an ankle slightly and discovered the healing powers of salt water; for an hour I sat at the water's edge, bathing my feet and massaging them with seaweed. It was wonderfully soothing, and took away the aching pain I had experienced all afternoon.

I remember that wee attic bedroom, where the Red One, uneasy in his sleep, turned round and brought down some plaster from the ceiling, causing me to forsake the bed and sleep on the floor.

In that house, too, we read again the story of Prince Charlie's wanderings in Skye. Every mile of that road from Uig to Snizort has some association with the '45, and the story never loses in the telling. Flora and the Prince set out from South Uist one dark summer night. Their six-oared boat—the "bonny boat" of song and story—was storm-tossed, and it was only after rowing hard all night that they landed at Monkstadt. Soldiers, searching for the Prince, were camping near by, but Lady Macdonald lent her aid and the whole party set off on foot towards Kingsburgh.

The glamour of romance was with us as we trekked south from Uig, following in their footsteps. The road climbs high up, and just beyond the school are the remains of a stone circle, much better marked than most of these relics of the past. Farther on, at

Earlish, we added to our collection of funny post-offices.

Soon we came to Glen Hinnisdale, but could not find the well where, tradition tells us, Prince Charlie quenched his thirst. The map has it marked about half-a-mile south of the bridge, by the side of the Lòn Ruadh, a tributary of the River Hinnisdal.

A little way farther south a road leads down to Kingsburgh, where the Prince sought shelter and was welcomed by The Macdonald. It was here that Flora approached timidly and was laughingly allowed to " cut ae lock frae his lang yellow hair." When Samuel Johnson visited the island Flora and her husband were living at Kingsburgh, and it was here the Englishman wrote of Flora : " A name that will be mentioned in history, and if courage and fidelity be virtue, mentioned with honour."

From Romesdal we could have ferried across Loch Snizort Beag, so shortening our journey by six or seven miles, but we preferred to keep to shank's nag. By the old kirk at Snizort we rested awhile, and decided that some time we would return and climb the Storr again by Glen Haultin. As no rock can be seen from this side, the whole ridge loses much of its impressiveness.

From Snizort the road leads back, through the clachan of Borve, to Portree. We turned south by a cart track which leads across the moor to Skeabost. The young folks of Skye know how to enjoy themselves. At the Skeabost post-office was a notice intimating a dance the following night at the " Garage " (ten years ago it would have been a barn). It was billed to start at 9.30 P.M. We saw many such notices on our journeyings; never once did we see any intimation as to when the dance would finish. You just " dance till ye drap," and go home with the milk.

From the bridge over the Snizort river can be seen a small island, which has an ancient burial-ground among the ruins of one of St Columba's churches.

Here we had a pleasant surprise, for in this road there are more trees than we had seen since landing in Skye. For a mile and a half the road, bordered by beech hedges, winds through woodlands. It was a welcome change from the naked moorland we had come to expect, and shows what could be done for Skye were afforestation carried out on a large scale.

We were at the hamlet of Bernisdale at half-past six and, feeling fine, decided to push on to Edinbain. From Bernisdale the road winds round the peninsula separating Loch Snizort Beag and Loch Greshornish. The map showed that Edinbain was almost due west, so we struck across country. The poor motorist, confined always to man-made roads, misses the best parts of the countryside. The distance across would be about four miles, and it was glorious to feel the springy heather beneath the feet after a day on the hard roads.

We thought we would be able to go straight across the moor, but when we glimpsed Loch Ravag we

knew we were too far inland, and had to climb Ben
Uigshader to get a fresh direction. It was late now,
and we were glad to see the silvery gleam of Loch
Greshornish, with Edinbain nestling at its head.
Our haven in sight, progress was much more rapid,
and soon we were sitting down to a substantial high-
tea at the inn.

(For alternative routes see page 106.)

CHAPTER VI

THE FAIRY BRIDGE, DUNVEGAN AND GLENDALE

> Let them sing of the sunny South,
>   Where the blue Ægean smiles.
> But give to me the Scottish sea
>   That breaks round the Western Isles!
> Jerusalem, Athens and Rome,
>   I would see them before I die!
> But I'd rather not see any one of the three,
>   Than be exiled for ever from Skye!
>
> NICOLSON.

DULL grey skies greeted us the next morning, and then the rain came down. . . .

We waited in the hope that it would clear off, but it only became heavier. Dunvegan Castle was open to visitors that afternoon, so, buckling on our capes, we set off. There were no vistas for us that day; the mists hung low and the Cuillin had retreated into the grey darkness. We made good progress over the Vaternish Ridge and down to the cross-roads at the Fairy Bridge, where three roads meet.

A tattered election poster on the wall of the road-men's hut—the only building within miles—shattered our dreams of fairies. What induced Sir Murdoch Macdonald to have bills posted on that isolated spot? Did he wish to invoke the aid of the fairies, who live, so they say, below green knolls on Ben Horneval, near by: those same fairies who, in days gone by, rallied to the cause of The MacLeod? For

47

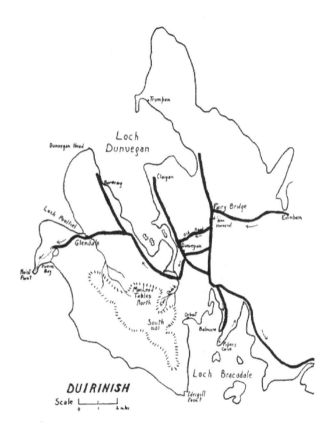

Trumpan

Loch
Dunvegan

Dunvegan Head

Borrodag

Claigan

Fairy Bridge

Edinbain

Loch Pooltiel

Old Road

Ben
Horneval

Glendale

Dunvegan

Neist
Point

Pooltiel
Bay

MacLeod's
Tables
North

South
1601

Orbost

Balmore

Pipers
Cave

Loch Bracadale

Idrigill
Point

DUIRINISH

Scale
0   1   6 miles

is there not preserved in Dunvegan Castle, to this day, a fairy flag, gifted to one of the chiefs by his fairy wife? And did she not give to the flag the power of three times succouring the clan when in danger? Twice, they say, and both times successfully, has the flag been waved in critical clan feuds. Small wonder, then, that even a prosaic M.P. should wish the help of such powerful allies!

We alas! saw no signs of fairies. But we did see a glen—a fairy glen. This one leaves the road about a mile south of the Fairy Bridge, winds across the moor and down the Dunvegan burn to the castle. Lined by hawthorn and fir-trees, bordered by ditches brimming over with ferns and wild flowers, and with honeysuckle and wild roses in full bloom, it is a fitting gateway to that hoary old castle. Praise be that it is not a motor road! This cart track is the old road, and was probably the one followed by old man Johnson on his famous journey.

It is impossible to keep dry for long when it rains in Skye, and by this time we were in that happy condition of being so thoroughly soaked that we could not become any wetter. What of that! We had before us another mile or two of merry squelching, then a wash, a change and a good high-tea.

The bleak building, the small windows and the crudely painted sign, " TEAS AND ACCOMMODATION," did not seem inviting. But inside all was warmth and homeliness, instant hot water and grand feeding— at three o'clock in the afternoon!

So refreshed, we trudged through the mud and

rain to the castle: " Ane stark strength biggit on ane craig." We should have liked to have come upon it in sunshine, but as we first saw it, with stormy clouds hanging low, rain lashing down, and the loch surrounding it on three sides frothy with white caps, the grim castle seemed in its more natural element.

How can I fitly describe this castle, whose very walls are hoary with tradition; whose story, half legend, is one of fairies, wild revels, ghastly murders and terrible clan feuds? I was more interested in the ancient relics: that immense two-handed sword of Rory Mòr's—what a warrior he must have been !— and the curious Dunvegan Cup, which Sir Walter introduces into *The Lord of the Isles*.

> " 'Fill me thè mighty cup,' he said,
> 'Erst owned by royal Somerled.' "

There is, too, the precious Fairy Flag, threadbare now, and those relics dear to the Jacobite heart, Prince Charlie's waistcoat and that lock of his " lang yellow hair " which Flora cut off at Kingsburgh.

No; Dunvegan cannot be described. It must be seen. It is in itself a history of Scotland, as from its walls looked down succeeding chiefs, each of whom could tell a hundred tales. Modern comfort has been introduced, but so deftly that it does not clash with the brooding spirit of the ages. Yet it was incongruous to find in the chieftain's hall, scene of a thousand ancient gatherings, a grand piano, a wireless set, and, lying on the table, a copy of *All*

Quiet on the Western Front. How Rory Mòr, gallant raider, would have loved that book!

We had a glimpse—and it was enough—of that awful pit into which poor wretches were thrown, and from which there was no return. What a place! . . .

We walked through the grounds of the castle, with the burn in spate and Rory Mòr's waterfall a miniature Niagara. The MacLeod must surely be a kindly soul. One may wander at will. Our hearts warmed to him when we saw, instead of the usual vindictive notice, " TRESPASSERS WILL BE PROSECUTED," only the kindly sign, " PLEASE KEEP TO THE PATHS SO AS TO AVOID WALKING ON YOUNG TREES." Scotland would indeed be a trampers' paradise were other landowners to do likewise.

Dreaming of the castle, and its glorious history of warrior chiefs, we were abruptly brought back to the present by finding the reigning chief's name among those in a list in the post-office applying for a gun licence. To think that a MacLeod, whose forefathers ruled as kings, killed without mercy and brooked no interference, should have to ask permission to shoot!

As we wandered round the village we came upon one of those satisfying shops which appear able to supply anything on earth. In its windows, boots, seidlitz powders, jumpers, tooth-brushes, black striped balls, tinned salmon, shirts, bananas, camera spools, loaves, books, hams, cigarettes, tea and silk stockings made an amazing pot-pourri.

The next morning was one of those mornings when the weather clerk seems to be swithering between sunshine and rain. In the end he sent both. It was dull to begin with, then came swift-changing skies, bright sunshine, fleeting clouds and sharp showers of rain. All was in keeping with the countryside we walked over.

We started early. We had a long day before us— to the westernmost headland of Skye. This is one of those roads, now becoming steadily fewer, which the round-trip bus tourist never goes near. It will be a good ten miles from Dunvegan to Neist Point. Throughout the whole long length of it we saw no motor-cars nor met with other walkers.

Now we were at the foot of MacLeod's Tables, which we saw first from the summit of the Storr and glimpsed many times on our way south. The story goes that a certain chief of Dunvegan once attended a royal banquet at Edinburgh. The King, James the Fifth, asked him if he could, in his Highland domain, show him such a well-spread table. The MacLeod boasted that he could show a table more magnificent by far than any in the south. When James sailed to the West Highlands with his fleet he visited Dunvegan, and The MacLeod made good his boast. At nightfall the chief led the King to the summit of this hill. A banquet fit for a king was laid out on its huge flat surface. " This," said the chief, " is my table larger and finer than yours, and," pointing to hundreds of clansmen bearing flaming torches, " these are my candlesticks."

First southwards by the schoolhouse to join the main road to Glendale, then over a hill and down to the loch-side at Skinidin. Here we added to our collection of post-offices and general stores. At Colbost we started to climb again, and stopped where the road forks, the right to Husabost and Boreraig and the left to Glendale.

Who has not heard of Boreraig, once the site of the famous piping school of the Macrimmons? They were wise in their time, these ancient chiefs of Dunvegan. Did they allow their pipers to practise near the castle? No; they sent them to school at Boreraig, eight miles away on the other side of the loch, so that the chief's ears might never be assailed by their embryo wailings. There they spent a long and stern noviciate, some even being condemned to practise in underground caves. Only the finished piper, the champion of champions, could go to Dunvegan and test his powers before his chief.

The Macrimmons were the hereditary pipers of the MacLeods, and, of course, in the beginning it was a fairy who gave them the gift of sweet music. A fairy princess who lived near the pipers' hollow at Boreraig fell in love with one of their clan, and gifted to him a silver chanter, thus making the Macrimmons the finest pipers of all time.

We took the hilly road to the west. As we climbed up we had better and better vistas of Loch Dunvegan and its many islands. Then, suddenly, as we breasted the summit of the road, Glendale and Loch Pooltiel lay before us.

The name, "The Deil's Pool," bears witness to a tragedy of long ago: once a Norwegian prince was drowned in the loch. A great many of the names in this district are of Norse origin. The proper name for MacLeod's Tables is Healaval More and Healaval Beg, meaning "The Great and Small Flagstone Fells," while Horneval means "Eagle Fell." Duirinish, like Minginish and Trotternish, is also a Norse name, meaning "Rocky Promontory."

We did not expect to find such a big village hidden away in this valley. Glendale carries a large crofting population—there are six or seven different townships—and seemed to us quite a prosperous place. There was a surprising amount of building going on. Few of the old insanitary thatched cottages remain, the majority have now been converted into stone buildings of the usual bare, bleak, small-windowed type. Each stands four square in its own patch of ground, with its own track, a quagmire after rain, leading down to the road.

Down by the loch-side there is a regular maze of roads. Secondary roads, the map dubs them. The Ordnance men in Skye are regular optimists. These roads are at least three grades poorer than the secondary roads of the mainland. After a false start, which nearly landed us at Milovaig, we returned and took the road to Waterstein. This is one of those roads, indifferent on the map, for which the tramper is always looking out. No motorist with any respect for his car would venture on that track.

Again we climbed over a hill (a Skye road can't

keep level for more than a hundred yards) and down to a loch. This is a fresh-water one, Loch Mòr, and near by is the hamlet of Waterstein, six houses almost exactly similar in appearance. The road and moorland now became rather mixed up. We sighted a notice-board. It read: " MOTOR-CARS MUST NOT GO BEYOND THIS POINT." No penalties were listed but—beyond was a considerable precipice.

After the usual weather-worn Skye houses, with their ill-kept surroundings, the buildings which comprise Neist Lighthouse positively sparkle. All are painted white, a brilliant gleaming white. The paths, fences and walls are in excellent condition, and I should say that this is one of the best-kept places on the island. It has a splendid situation on the hump-backed headland, exposed to all the winds that blow. This lighthouse is the only one on the mainland of Skye. Till it was built, twenty-five years ago, the rocky coast was the scene of many shipwrecks. Now it is a friendly beacon, and the lighthouse man noted the increased traffic with the big liners which pass by during their short cruises to the Hebrides.

A tent and a food-supply for several days would be necessary before one could explore properly this part of Skye. The cliff scenery around is superb. Idrigill Point cannot be seen, but there is a majestic sweep of cliffs straight from the water's edge, round Moonen Bay to the Hoe Rape (the High Sea Cliff). Where burns find their way to the sea, waterfalls are formed and the cliffs are burrowed by innumerable caves.

The nearest bay is Camas nan Sithein (the Bay of the Fairies), and there is a Fairies' Cave underneath the waterfall where the burn from Loch Mòr tumbles into the sea.

We sat on the rocks in front of the lighthouse and gazed across the waters to the Blue Isles of the Hebrides we shall visit some day. Then, suddenly, the laughing summer sea darkened, stormy clouds hid the sun and lashing rain drove us to shelter. Ten minutes later the sky was blue again, the wet rocks glistened in the sun and the far western isles beckoned to us once more.

We spent most of the afternoon on the headland and returned to Dunvegan in the evening. There were no possible short cuts, and the road seemed much longer. An ominous mist hid MacLeod's Tables and a dull angry sunset prepared us for rain on the morrow.

Storm-bound in Dunvegan. . . .

Outside the trees were swaying wildly, the wet earth was heavy with the scent of peat, and the loch, whipped up by the wind, was a swaying mass of white.

But we were well content, close drawn up to a big peat fire. Nor was the day wasted. We composed between us the scenario of a talking film, *The Fairy Flag*. Here it is.

First there will be a glimpse of the Black Cuillin. Then will come the sound of a galloping horse, and the chief's son will appear on his way home to Dunvegan. While riding through a wood he hears elfin music and dismounts to investigate. He leads his horse deeper and deeper into the wood and finds the Fairy Queen holding her Court below an old oak-tree.

He watches for a while. The instincts of the raider prevail. He runs forward, seizes the Queen, throws her in front of his saddle and rides hard for Dunvegan. To ensure the good will of the fairies the old chief commands instant marriage. At the wedding ceremony emissaries of the fairies suddenly appear and present to the chief's son the fairies' gift, a silken flag. This the Fairy Queen endows with the power of three times rescuing the clan when in great danger.

Then there is feasting and high revelry in the castle. Glimpses of the kitchens, with oxen and sheep being roasted whole in huge fireplaces; of the chieftain's hall and the table groaning beneath the weight of foodstuffs. There will be jesting and dancing. Kilted men will dance reels with fair ladies and the Macrimmon himself will be piping. Outside there will be games for the clansmen: fighting with those ancient two-handed swords, wrestling and caber-tossing.

The scene changes. The Macdonalds are raiding the MacLeods' lands in Bracadale. A village is fired, men put to the sword, women and cattle carried off. A wounded MacLeod escapes and, weary and blood-stained, carries the tidings to Dunvegan.

The clarion call to battle goes through the castle! Horses are saddled! Dirks and swords are sharpened!

Wild cries — galloping horses — terror - stricken villages!

Down by Drynoch and Sligachan goes the relentless pursuit. The Macdonalds retreat through Glen Sligachan. The MacLeods follow. There will be glimpses of their scouts climbing the great crags of Sgurr nan Gillean.

At Harta Corrie the Macdonalds turn, and prepare to give battle. Their vantage-point is well chosen and they hold off the MacLeods. Tired after their long pursuit, the battle goes against the men of Dunvegan.

When all seems lost the chief remembers the fairy's promise and waves aloft the fairy flag. To the Macdonalds it seems as if the ranks of the MacLeods have been increased fourfold. They turn and flee in confusion down by Coruisk. At the Bloody Stone a last stand is made—wild cries of the victors—agonized shrieks of the wounded—a fight to the death!

The MacLeods return to Dunvegan. Again there is high revelry in the castle.

Years pass. The old chief dies. The young chief rules in his stead. There comes a tragic time when his heir, a babe, is sick unto death. Messengers are sent out. Wise men, skilled in healing, are brought from the mainland. But all of no avail. The child is dying. The mother is wild with despair. A clansman suggests that the aid of the fairies should be again invoked. The treasured flag is brought out and waved aloft. The baby recovers. The succession is assured. The flag now becomes an object of reverence, and a brave family of the clan are appointed its hereditary keepers.

Try as we might we could not conceive a fitting finish for our story. There must be an epic incident when the flag is waved for the third and last time.

Who will be the film producer brave enough to go to Skye and "take" this story? What sets he could have at Dunvegan, the oldest inhabited house in Britain, and what a background the Cuillin would make for a clan fight by the lone dark waters of Coruisk!

(For alternative routes see page 107.)

CHAPTER VII

LOCH BRACADALE—CLAN FEUDS—CARBOST

> The grey mists shadow-drifting,
> The scent of rain-sweet heather,
> The cloud-white wander-weather.

SOUTHWARDS from Dunvegan we had the best walking day of all. A day's heavy rain had left the country-side sweet and fresh, with the homely reek of the peat and the scent of bog-myrtle pervading the air. All day long we were either climbing hills from loch to loch, or walking by a loch-side, with ever-changing views of sea, loch, land and mountains around us, and the mighty Cuillin in front beckoning us on.

We passed by the ancient burial-ground where lie generations of MacLeods. One remembers the haunting verses of Dr Lachlan MacLean Watt, himself a native of Skye.

> " Land of the brave and proud,
> When I lie all still in my shroud,
> O bury me in Dunvegan,
> In the country of MacLeod.
>
> Cold is the town and street,
> And the faces that here I meet,
> And I long for old Dunvegan
> With the Gaelic and the peat.

So carry me home to Skye,
Where the Cuillin are wild and high,
And the sea sings round Dunvegan,
And the place where the dear ones lie."

We were often reminded of The MacLeod's domain. It was long before those flat-topped hills, his " Tables," disappeared from view, and many times we glimpsed, over at Idrigill Point, those rocky pillars, " MacLeod's Maidens." Once, they say, the wife and daughter of a certain chief were drowned here, when their galley was wrecked. There are three pillars in all, known as the mother and her two daughters.

About two miles south of Dunvegan we first saw the silvery gleam of Loch Bracadale, with its floating islands. At Roskhill we left the main road and took the old road which leads south to the Vatten Peninsula. Two miles took us to Balmore, where the road ends. We continued past the ruins of an old church, and a mound marking the situation of an ancient dun, to Harlosh Point. Our object was a visit to the famous Piper's Cave.

Our walk was in vain. The tide was nearly full, and it was impossible to descend to the foot of the cliffs. We could just see the entrance to the cave, which is near a big rock pillar on the east side of the point.

This is the cave which the piper, playing the pipes, marched into and never returned. As he disappeared into the blackness he exclaimed: " I doot, I doot, I'll ne'er come oot." So the story goes, and they say that the cave finishes ten miles north, at Greshornish Point, on Loch Snizort.

Most of the Skye caves have such stories and such legendary tunnels attached to them. Strathaird has its Spar Cave, sometimes called Cave of Gold, while Portree has its Piper's Cave, with a similar story to the Harlosh one.

From the point we had a grand view of the rugged headlands, Rudha nan Clach and Idrigill, which form the portals of Loch Bracadale. Near at hand are the islands of Harlosh, Tarner and Wiay, each with its own cliffs and caves. We could see the caves at Orbost Point, and many others between Loch Varkasaig and Idrigill Point, the whole coastline here being honeycombed with them. The best way to visit them is by the sea, and a motor-boat can be hired at Balmore. We returned up by the east side of Vatten. The map has several " Tumuli " marked about here. These are just heaps of stones, and are supposed to be the burial-places of the very early inhabitants of the island.

Somewhere near here is the site of one of the clan fights between the MacLeods and the Macdonalds. These places are almost as numerous as Prince Charlie's Caves! They were mighty warriors, these Celts, and fighting was their very life-blood. It is difficult to decide which of the two clans was the more cruel and bloodthirsty. Probably the Mac-Leods would win, but only because they had their headquarters at Dunvegan all through the centuries, and so have a more complete history.

Once the MacLeods discovered a large gathering of Macdonalds in a cave on the island of Eigg. This was too good an opportunity to miss. They built a huge fire at the entrance and suffocated them all to death.

Many years passed by. The Macdonalds did not forget. One black Sunday they landed at Ardmore, in Vaternish, while the MacLeods were worshipping in the near-by church of Trumpan. They fired the building and burned alive men, women and children. Only one woman escaped. Quickly she raised the clan, and they converged on Trumpan. The Macdonalds tried to escape, only to find that the tide had gone out, leaving their galleys stranded high and dry. They were forced to give battle, and few escaped death. The MacLeods did not bother to give the dead proper burial: they just laid them alongside a dyke which separated the field from the shore, and tumbled the stones over the bodies. Only afterwards did it occur to the MacLeods that the sea would now encroach on their land, so for all time that fight was known as " The Battle of the Spoiled Dykes."

When it came to " bumping off " inconvenient folks these ancient chiefs had nothing to learn from modern Chicago gunmen. A right good hand-to-hand fight they enjoyed, but did not hesitate to use the poisoned cup, the deadly dirk, the loathsome dungeon.

Some figures stand out. Of one—Donald Gorme of Duntulm—there are many stories. A kinsman, by name Hugh, plotted to murder him. Donald learned of the plot, invited the unsuspecting man to the castle, and straightway threw him into the dungeon. Now and then he fed him with salt beef, till Hugh went raging mad and died of thirst.

This same Macdonald married a sister of The MacLeod. There was no divorce in those days; the usual method of treating an unwanted wife was just to put her into the dungeon and forget all about her. This was much too simple for Donald; moreover his good lady had but one eye, and he himself was spoiling for a fight, so he sent her back to Dunvegan, mounted on a one-eyed pony, led by a one-eyed man and followed by a one-eyed dog! No chief could withstand such an insult. Instantly clan war broke out.

Not long afterwards The MacLeod looked out from the windows of Dunvegan one wild, stormy night and said that even if his worst enemy sought shelter he could not refuse to let him in. That very night Donald Gorme, returning from a raid, had his galley forced into Loch Dunvegan, and almost wrecked, near the castle. He showed his iron nerve when he walked boldly to the door and sought shelter for himself and his followers.

The MacLeod made good his promise, took them in and fed them. He then gave the Macdonalds the use of an outbuilding for the night. An hour or two later, when he thought them all asleep, he set fire to the building, only to find that the crafty Donald, anticipating just such a fate, had already escaped with his men out of the windows!

Then there was a certain MacLeod, Black Iain, who made himself chief by murdering uncles, cousins, brothers, and brought a reign of terror to Dunvegan. This was the chief who once invited eleven Campbell chieftains to a banquet at the castle. At the table each Campbell was seated between two MacLeods. The feast over, a bowl of blood was brought in and placed before the chief. This was the sign. Each MacLeod stabbed to death the Campbell on his right!

Black Iain lived cruelly and died cruelly—by having a red-hot poker thrust into his stomach.

Then there was Rory Mòr—Sir Rory, the first MacLeod to be knighted by a Scottish king—a mighty and well-loved warrior, of whom countless tales are told.

And so down through the centuries. Battle, murder, and sudden death!

Yet the clans were but living the normal life of those days. Cruel? Of course they were cruel! They had to be cruel. The clansmen expected cruelty. The chiefs reigned by cruelty—and the strength of their sword arm. Any sign of weakness and there was a kinsman ready and eager to commit murder and take the chief's place.

In quieter times at home the fighting spirit found its outlet in the Empire's battles all over the world. The Highlanders from Skye were first-class fighting men, and were ever in the forefront of battle. Many rose to high rank; it is said that one branch of the MacLeods had at the same time two generals in the British Army.

Iain Breac MacLeod, son of the twenty-third chief,

last male heir in direct line, died fighting, at Ypres, in 1915.

. . . . . .

At the head of Loch Caroy is a little, deserted church which will some time disappear; the sea is encroaching steadily, and already part of the churchyard has crumbled and fallen into the loch.

Just beyond this, a dream of mine came true. Since coming to Skye the haunting refrain of *The Canadian Boat Song* had been in my mind, and there, by the roadside, I saw what I like to think was the original "lone shieling." The exile's vision must have been of one such as this:

" From the lone shieling on the misty island,
    Mountains divide us and the waste of seas;
 Yet still the blood is warm, the heart is Highland,
    And we in dreams behold the Hebrides.
 Fair these broad meads, these hoary woods are grand,
    But we are exiles from our fathers' land."

It is interesting to note that during the Scott Centenary celebrations, last year, several writers claimed that Sir Walter was the author of these words. On his brief visit to Skye he sailed from Dunvegan to Loch Scavaig; the only "lone shielings " he saw on the island would be in the vicinity of Dunvegan.

From Loch Caroy the road keeps inland for four miles over the moor to Loch Beag, another arm of Loch Bracadale. Beyond Struan we climbed up the hillside to visit Dun Beag, the best preserved of all he ancient Skye forts and a splendid viewpoint.

Photo

NEIST LIGHTHOUSE

B. H. Humble

[Facing page 80

Photo

A LONE SHIELING IN SKYE

W. J. MacArthur

[Facing page 67

About here a lonely road leads off across the moors to Portree, nine miles away. The main road, after passing Bracadale kirk, winds down to the loch-side. When the tide is low it is possible to wade across the head of the loch, so cutting off a mile or two.

Then there is a long pull uphill and a hilly road to Drynoch. The next six miles are well inland, and out of sight of water. Good foot-men now, we kept up a steady four miles per hour. We were in good spirits because the Cuillin, our Mecca, were drawing nearer, and now and then the elusive mist would rise from the brae faces and reveal their splintered masses cutting the sky.

At Drynoch we left the main road and waded across the river to the Glen Brittle road. Feeling fine, we thought of pushing on to Loch Brittle, but Carbost, immortalized in Maurice Walsh's *The Key above the Door*, that book of the heather, drew us like a magnet.

For Carbost is the Uiskavagh of the story. Here came Tom King—Long Tom King of Loch Ruighi —to meet that " devil of an Irishman," Neil Quinn, and in his gay company forgot certain happenings on the ruddy wine moors of the province of Moray. Here did King gather again the lost threads of his life. Quinn gave the prescription:

" There is a breeze across the heather finer than the finest usquebaugh. You will take to the moors, my father, and let the sun and wind work on you. The Cuillin will be watching you on the one hand

and the uncaring sea will be taking no notice of
you on the other, and the cloud shadows will be
racing across the hills as they have raced for these
eighty or eight hundred million years. All these
things make for serenity—go thou and acquire it."

With them we trudged the moors when they had
" a wallop at the Cuillin and a peep down at Coruisk,
that dark lost water."

No; Carbost is not the place one can pass by.
And Carbost seemed to expect us. We did not even
have to inquire about lodgings. The lad at the
post-office asked us at once if we wished a room
for the night, and then went across the road and
arranged things for us.

Afterwards we wandered up the hillside where
the War Memorial stands. Though it is only ten
years old, it is already so weather-beaten as to make
the lettering almost indecipherable. Surely there
must be some special quality in the Skye weather.
We noticed the same in the appearance of the
memorials at Broadford and Portree.

In the days of old, castles were built on carefully
chosen sites, commanding all approaches. No less
care was taken when churches were built, the only
difference being to make them more accessible.
Now the War Memorials of Skye, especially of the
smaller villages, occupy commanding sites, and can
be seen afar off. The position of the Carbost one
could not be bettered. We agreed that the best
situated of them all was that cross, dedicated to the
" Men of Sleat," on a rocky headland of Knock Bay.

In the early evening the Cuillin, to the south, were shrouded in a dense, dirty yellow mist, just like a bad Glasgow fog. Later, as happened so often, the mist lifted, leaving the whole mighty range, steel-blue that night, standing out against a cloudless sky.

Carbost was the only place where we met fellow-trampers. We sat long round the peat fire in the kitchen, and talked and talked. These two had stories to tell of three weeks' wanderings in Ross and Cromarty, and were setting off at five o'clock the following morning to catch the bus at Sligachan for Kyle and the south.

(For alternative routes see page 109.)

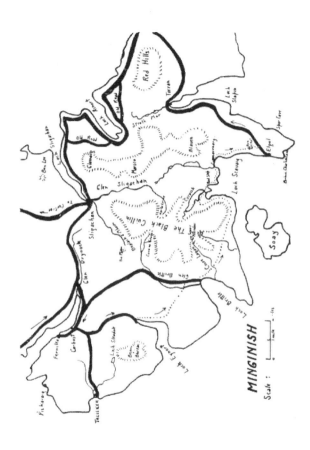

MINGINISH

Scale:

CHAPTER VIII

GLEN BRITTLE AND THE CUILLIN

Gray winding glen with long grasses blowing,
  Swept by the storm wind and wet with the rain;
Burns spraying high in the rush of their flowing,
  What would I give now to know you again!
Hills of my heart, you have charms for beguiling
  All of God's world and his heavens above;
Stern to the stranger, bleak and unsmiling,
  Bleak, but how dear to me—hills that I love.

GRAHAM DALLAS.

So, with the Cuillin in front, we faced southwards.
Our route lay, by a rough cart track, up the Carbost
burn, over the hill and down to lonely Loch Eynort.
We met no one by the way. Yet once these hills
echoed the cries of the clansmen; it was here the
Macdonalds landed from their galleys before the
battle of Coire na Creiche. From the top of the loch
we followed a path along its eastern shore, for about
two miles, to the red-roofed cottage of Kraiknish.
From here the map shows a path winding over the
hills to Loch Brittle. We were able to follow it for
a short distance and then, as paths have a habit of
doing in Skye, it disappeared, leaving us marooned
on the moorland. We kept on to the top of the ridge
and then threw ourselves down on the heather.

Below us lay the long curve of Glen Brittle, the
road winding by the river, and, at the loch-side, a
few crofts and a gleaming stretch of golden sands;

beyond, heather slopes rose up to great gullies and black crags fading into the mist. We scrambled down through the heather and across the river to the roadside opposite Coire na Banachdich.

Again good fortune was with us. We at once secured accommodation at the post-office, which receives mails twice a week and has no telephone. Other than to climbers Glen Brittle is hardly known; there are only three cottages available and they are usually booked up by hillmen for the summer months. Cragsmen are drawn to Glen Brittle year after year, and the visitors' books in the cottages contain many well-known names. The casual walker cannot count on getting accommodation during July and August.

Yet to the tramper who knows nothing of rock-climbing Glen Brittle is ideal for a holiday, provided he has an experienced leader when he tries the rock. Even if he keeps clear of the great mountains altogether there are other attractions. Beinn an Eòin (the Bird Mount, 1023) and An Cruachan (1423) are good viewpoints, while there are fine walks round by the sea-cliffs either towards Loch Eynort or Gars-bheinn. Coire Lagan and Coir' a' Ghrundha are two of the grandest Cuillin corries and, particularly after rain, there are beautiful water-falls on the burns coming from Coire Ghreadaidh (pron. *Greeta*) and Coire na Banachdich. There is boating, bathing and fishing; Coruisk—that dark water—to visit, and over all the abiding silence of old places and the brooding mystery of the mountains.

We were glad we had left to the last this part of Skye, of which Sir Walter wrote: " rivals in grandeur and desolate sublimity anything that the Highlands can produce."

They say that when God made the world He had His hands full of mountains and, when over Skye, dropped some—hence the Black Cuillin.

For ten days they had been calling us, and now we were at their feet. Their attraction was irresistible: we could not wait till the morrow so went off that evening and climbed the lower spur of Sgurr Dearg. The mist hung low, and we watched it swirling across that wild corrie, rising and falling, revealing momently the shattered crags above. We did not go far, because, though bright and warm in the valley, it was bitterly cold even on the lower ridge.

We came down by one of the scree slopes which are so common on the Skye mountains. To the uninitiated I would explain that scree is a long, steep stretch of loose stones on the hillside. These may be as fine as gravel or as large as rocks. Tackling screes is an art. When crossing them slowness spells disaster, you will slide down two or three feet for every foot across. The bigger the stones the greater the care required, and to climb up behind the leader is to risk a broken head. On this one, composed of small stones, we were able to run down. It was exhilarating, and the whole hillside seemed to move down with us.

We looked out early next morning and shouted

with joy when we saw the high Cuillin clear to their
tops and the great peaks piercing a sky still aglow in
the blaze of a rising sun. A grand day for a climb!
Our luck still held good.   This, the day we had
chosen for the mountains, was just such another day
as we had for the ridge walk from Portree to Staffin,
a very paradise of a day.

Early in the forenoon we set off, crossed the river
and climbed up through the heather and the lichen-
covered rocks.   There must have been very special
fairies in Glen Brittle, for the lochan on the hillside,
Loch an Fhir-bhallaich, means " The Loch of the
Spotted Folk."   Passing it we turned into Coire
Lagan (the Corrie of the Hollows).   It was a grand
scramble up the burn to its source, a lovely little
lochan, 1800 feet up, imprisoned between the
mountain giants. The name, " a wild gem among
the Cuillin," which has been applied to Coruisk, I
would rather have given to Lochan Coire Lagan.
For so it seemed that glorious day.   It is worth
visiting by non-climbers and would be a fine spot
for a picnic.   The route is certainly rough, but could
be done by any normal person.

We rested for a while on the hot rocks and watched
three cragsmen set off to " do " the round of Coire
Lagan.   This is a favourite ridge walk, and means
topping, in succession, Sgurr Sgumain, Alaisdair,
Thearlaich, Mhic Coinnich and Dearg.   They
started for Sgumain, and soon loose stones came
clattering down.

After taking some photographs we commenced

the climb of Sgurr Alaisdair by the Great Stone Shoot. It is just that! A shoot, 1300 feet long, the longest stretch of scree in Britain, of loose stones of all sizes running up at a very steep angle between Sgurr Alaisdair and Sgurr Thearlaich. It means using hands and feet all the time, as often you will slide one step downwards for two steps upwards. It is not difficult, and any climber should be able to get to the top of the Shoot.

We were heartily glad to get to the top and throw ourselves down for a breather. Lochan Coire Lagan cannot be seen from here, but Lochan Coir' a'Ghrundha lies below to the south. Seton Gordon has described it as the loveliest of all mountain lochans. We could not agree. It is wild and gloomy and certainly not lovely. Rather does Lochan Coire Lagan, on the day we saw it, merit his description.

Lochan Coir' a' Ghrundha (the Lochan of the Floor Corrie—probably because of the amount of rock debris) is at a height of 2300 feet, and the tramper who eschews the peaks will find it well worth a visit. The corrie is steeper and gives much stiffer scrambling than Coire Lagan. The burn tumbles down by a series of waterfalls, and the best route of ascent is on its north side.

From the top of the Shoot to the peak there is a little rock-work which must be taken carefully. Soon we stood on the highest point in Skye and placed stones on the top of the cairn. The mountain is named after Sheriff Alexander Nicolson, that lover of Skye, who did so much to make the wonders

of the Cuillin known and who is the author of those
well-known lines:

> " Lovest thou mountains great,
>   Peaks to the clouds that soar,
>   Corrie and fell where eagle dwell,
>   And cataracts dash evermòre?
>   Lovest thou green grassy glades,
>   By the sunshine sweetly kist,
>   Murmuring waves and echoing caves?
>   Then go to the Isle of Mist."

He it was who first climbed it (1873). He describes
it thus: " The climb on the other side of the corrie
(Coire Lagan) was stiff and warm and some judg-
ment was required to find a way, and still more
when it came to circumventing the peak. We did
it, however, without much difficulty; one or two
places were somewhat trying, requiring good grip
of hands and feet but, on the whole, I have seen
worse places."

The summit itself is so slender that there is only
room for one person to stand beside the cairn at a
time, but just beyond, to the west, is a spot where
four or five people can sit down. The view from here
on a clear day is one of the finest in all Scotland.
Green Soay seems quite near, and beyond are the
islands whose names appeal to the thirsty one: Rum,
Eigg and Canna. Farther off is the whole stretch
of the Hebrides and, on the horizon, little dark spots
mark the position of the Lone Isles of St Kilda, a
hundred miles away. It is the mountains which
attract most. We could trace the whole ridge from

Sgurr Mhic Coinnich   Sgurr Thearlaich   Top of Great Stone Shoot   Sgurr Alasdair

Photo   *A. E. Robertson*

SGURR ALAISDAIR AND SGURR MHIC COINNICH FROM SGURR DEARG SHOWING GREAT STONE SHOOT

[Facing page 76

Sgurr-an-Sradhidh

Photo

LOCH CORUISK AND LOCH SCAVAIG FROM SGURR À'MHADAIDH

A. E. Robertson

[Facing page 77

Gars-bheinn in the south to Sgurr nan Gillean away in the north. What names they have! We can spell them, but that, alas, gives no hint whatever as to the method of pronunciation! Here are the names and approximate heights (from south to north):

Gars-bheinn (2934). The Echoing Mountain.

Sgurr nan Eag (3037). The Notched Peak.

Sgurr Dubh na Da Bheinn (3069). The Black Peak of the Two Hills.

Sgurr Dubh Mòr (3089). The Big Black Peak.

Sgurr Sgumain (3104). The Stack Peak.

Sgurr Alaisdair (3309). Alexander's Peak.

Sgurr Thearlaich (3201). Charles's Peak, named after that doughty climber, Charles Pilkington.

Sgurr Mhic Coinnich (3107). Mackenzie's Peak, after John of that ilk, the famous guide.

Sgurr Dearg (3234). The Red Peak.

Sgurr na Banachdich (3167). The Milkmaid's Peak.

Sgurr Thormaid (3040). Norman's Peak, after another climber of the early days, Professor Norman Collie.

Sgurr a' Ghreadaidh (3197). The Peak of Mighty Winds.

Sgurr a' Mhadaidh (3010). The Foxes' Peak.

Bidein Druim nan Ramh (2850). The Peak of the Ridge of Oars.

Bruach na Frithe (3143). The Brae of the Forest.

Sgurr a' Fionn Choire (3065). The Peak of the White Corrie.

Am Basteir (3070). The Executioner.

Sgurr nan Gillean (3167). The Peak of Ghylls or Gullies.

We knew the mountains now, and could pick out most of them without the aid of a map. There was the giant mass of Blaven (3042), the Red Hills we had travelled through, and away to the north was the Storr, and the ridge which gave us our climbing baptism in Skye.

It seems incredible that such mountains as these should have been left in isolation till the latter half of the nineteenth century. All the Alpine giants were conquered before the Cuillin. By the natives they were deemed unclimbable, and it was only about 1870 that they aroused interest. The supposed "inaccessible pinnacle" of Sgurr Dearg was climbed for the first time by the Pilkingtons in 1880. Nowadays this crazy pillar is regularly climbed in many different ways and hillmen all over Britain sing the praises of the good gabbro rock of the Cuillin.

Almost every possible climb has now been explored, but the cragsman will tell you that that does not matter, and will speak enthusiastically of the grand joy of grappling with "the grey brown ledges." After a first taste of the Cuillin, on a good summer day, many walkers will be eager to learn the technicalities of the climbing game. Skye can offer them every phase. There, under good leadership, they can graduate from easier climbs to gullies and chimneys which have tested to the utmost some of the best climbers of our time.

As we lay on the peak we saw three climbers, roped together, appear over the top of Sgurr

Sgumain and start to negotiate that tricky ridge between it and Alaisdair. This ridge is a narrow wall in parts, with a sheer drop on either side and a *mauvais pas*. They took it slowly and carefully. After a while we lost sight of them and a short time later the leader's head appeared at our feet.

There were now five of us on the peak and the accommodation was taxed to its utmost. It was the first good climbing day for a week and there were many climbers on the hills. The first party moved on, and we watched a second party do the Sgumain-Alaisdair ridge.

How long we stayed on the peak I know not. Hours fly past quickly on the mountains, and such was the glory of that perfect day that we were in no hurry to return to the lowlands. At last, reluctantly, we started downwards, and found the descent of the Great Stone Shoot much easier than its ascent. We took it slowly on our return down the burn, but from the mouth of the corrie our pace improved, for we had the climber's hunger.

Such was our first day on the high Cuillin, a never-to-be-forgotten day. And the talk that night was all of screes, ledges, gullies, cracks, and chimneys, and what we would do—some day.

Fittingly, a perfect sunset followed a perfect day. The great mountains remained clear to their tops and the sky in the west was ablaze with glory.

It is interesting to note that on more than one occasion all the highest Cuillin peaks have been climbed in one day. This means seven miles to and from the ridges and eight miles on the ridges, the whole traverse involving about 10,000 feet of ascent. It is usually done from south to north, by starting at dawn from Glen Brittle, climbing Gars-bheinn, following the ridge the whole way to Sgurr nan Gillean and finishing at Sligachan. Only skilled cragsmen in perfect physical condition could accomplish such a feat. F. S. Smythe, of Himalayan fame, has often climbed in Skye, and is one of the select few who have done the whole ridge in one day. This occurred several years ago, Smythe's companion being J. H. B. Bell, the well-known Scottish climber.

(For alternative routes see page 109.)

CHAPTER IX

CORUISK, CAMASUNARY, ELGOL

The mem'ry conjures up your riven summits,
  Your sculptured crags and wildly rushing streams;
We seek you still, oh, far-off, well-loved Cuillin,
    In waking dreams.

L. P. Abraham.

Our holiday was nearing a close now and, much as we wished it, we could not give another day to the mountains. We left Glen Brittle with Elgol as our destination. Had the day been fine we might have ventured over one of the bealachs to Coruisk, but mist, a hint of rain and the weight of our packs kept us to the lowlands.

We started at noon, and, keeping about a hundred feet up, skirted right round the mountains. This area collects all the water from the southern Cuillin, so we were squelching through bogs most of the time. We travelled slowly, and it took us a good three hours to get near Coruisk.

As we rounded Gars-bheinn we saw the steamer enter Loch Scavaig and drop anchor. What a poor way to visit this loch of lochs—a crowded steamer and a half-mile walk to the shore of Coruisk! Coruisk will be the better appreciated if it is the reward after a hard trek through the desolation of Glen Sligachan or round the mountains from Glen Brittle. The Red One spoke my mind when he said: " We don't want to go down there and find a lot of tourists. That would spoil it all." We rested, then continued farther inland, across the Allt a' Chaoich (the Mad Burn) and eventually climbed down by the lower crags of Sgurr Dubh to the loch-side.

It was late afternoon. All tourists had long departed. We were alone in the vast solitude. The loch, hemmed in by walls of rock, was gloomy and awesome. For a moment the mist lifted from Druim nan Ramh and Sgurr a' Mhadaidh and a stray gleam of sunshine brightened the murky waters.

Sir Walter Scott described it thus:

> " For rarely human eye has known
>   A scene so stern as that dread lake
>   With its dark ledge of barren stone."

We went southwards, over the stepping-stones in the River Scavaig and to the large boulder from where the loch is usually viewed. Here have come many whose names are famous in literature and who have left on record pen-pictures of the scene. But cold print will never suffice to describe Coruisk. Yet it was with something of a thrill we took photographs from the spot where Sir Walter Scott first saw the loch.

First impressions are lasting, and the weather will have much to do with one's remembrance of Coruisk. In bright sunshine, with the mountains clear to the tops, gloominess gives place to rugged grandeur, and then one appreciates that description of Coruisk— " a beautiful gem among the Cuillin."

Sir Walter must obviously have seen the loch on a dull day, and from where he stood he could not see that oasis of greenery at the north end of the loch which was once the site of a mountaineering camp.

Yet, out of all the writers, he alone managed to convey, in prose and in verse, something of the spirit of this wild place. Sir Walter landed at Loch Scavaig and walked to Coruisk. In his own personal diary he records it thus: "Advancing up this huddling and riotous brook, we found ourselves in a most extraordinary scene: we were surrounded by hills of the boldest and most precipitous character, and on the margin of a lake which seemed to have sustained the constant ravages of torrents from these rude neighbours. The shores consisted of huge layers of naked granite, here and there intermixed with bogs and heaps of gravel and sand marking the course of the torrents. Vegetation there was little or none, and the mountains rose so perpendicularly from the water's edge that Borrowdale is a jest to them. I never saw a spot on which there was less appearance of vegetation of any kind; the eye rested on nothing but brown and naked crags, and the rocks on which we walked by the side of the loch were as bare as the pavement of Cheapside."

In *The Lord of the Isles* Scott makes Bruce land here. Said Ronald:

> " If true mine eye,
> These are the savage wilds that lie
> North of Strathnardill and Dunskye;
>   No human foot comes here,
> What hinders that on land we go
>   And strike a mountain deer? "

Bruce agrees. They land, and reach Coruisk.
Said Bruce:

" ' I've traversed many a mountain-strand,
    Abroad and in my native land,
    And it has been my lot to tread
    Where safety more than pleasure led;
    Thus, many a waste I've wandered o'er,
    Clombe many a crag, cross'd many a moor,
        But, by my halidome!
    A scene so rude, so wild as this,
    Yet so sublime in barrenness,
    Ne'er did my wandering footsteps press,
        Where'er I happ'd to roam.'

            .   .   .   .   .

    The wildest glen, but this, can show
    Some touch of Nature's genial glow;
    On high Benmore green mosses grow,
    And heath-bells bud in deep Glencroe,
        And copse on Cruchan-Ben;
    But here,—above, around, below,
        On mountain or in glen,
    Nor tree, nor shrub, nor plant, nor flower,
    Nor aught of vegetative power,
        The weary eye may ken."

We walked down to the so-called "Port" on
Loch Scavaig. There are no buildings at Port
Sgaile (the Port of Refuge), only a landing-place on
the rocks, and iron rings for tying up the boats.

Tourists are brought over to Loch Scavaig from
Elgol by motor-boat, so the tired walker may, if lucky,
find room in the boat for the return journey. It is
much better to continue the walk round the coast.

Every map has the "Bad Step" clearly marked.

References to it are so frequent in books on Skye that we expected to find a sensational ledge above the sea. But it was in the olden days, when the Cuillin were regarded as impregnable, that it received its name, from pedestrians who counted its passing an achievement. Only on windy and stormy days would it be difficult to pass. A boatman showed us the best place to cross the rock, about fifteen feet above sea-level. It can be avoided altogether by climbing a little way up the hillside.

The path to Camasunary is fairly well marked, and as we rounded Rudha Bàn, " Blaven, rocky Blaven," came into view once more. Blaven was always Alexander Smith's favourite mountain, and he sang of it:

> " O Blaven, rocky Blaven,
>   How I long to be with you again,
>   To see lashed gulf and gully
>   Smoke white in the windy rain—
>   To see in the scarlet sunrise
>   The mist-wreaths perish with heat,
>   The wet rock slide with a trickling gleam
>   Right down to the cataract's feet."

Camasunary is the English version of Camas Fhionnairidh (the Bay of the Beautiful Shieling). Stepping-stones lead across the river which comes from Loch na Creitheach (the Loch of Brushwood). After rain these may be covered. The cottage at Camasunary must surely be one of the loneliest habitations in the island. It has no communication by road. It stands by the water's edge, with a stretch of white sands before it and green fields around it. Northwards, a wild path winds through Strath na Creitheach to Sligachan; eastwards, there is a track over the hills to Loch Slapin, and four miles to the south is the nearest village, Elgol.

Alexander Smith, during his "summer in Skye," visited Camasunary. He tells how from Ord in Sleat he rowed across to Kilmarie in Strathaird, walked over the hills to Camasunary, and rowed from there to Port Sgaile. His companion talked of anchoring a floating hotel in Loch Scavaig. That was about eighty years ago! Since then others have remarked what a splendid situation there is for an hotel at Camasunary. It would be a desecration to build a modern hotel here. Let us hope that there will never be roads in this part of Skye; that the shores of Scavaig will be left for all time in splendid isolation for the walker. Maybe some time, when the Scottish Youth Hostels Association gets a footing in Skye, there will be a trampers' hostel at Camasunary.

Two fine ponies were grazing outside the cottage, and we found their owners—fishermen—ensconced in the kitchen with the keeper and his family. We were made welcome, and mightily refreshed by a pot of good Skye tea. One of the kiddies was sickly, and we were entrusted with a note to the postmaster at Elgol, who would phone for a doctor. We never discovered how the children got any schooling; in winter this cottage must be entirely isolated for days at a time.

We watched the fishermen zigzag up the hill and then set off southwards. Though we received minute instructions from the keeper we soon lost the path, and saw little of it the whole way to Elgol. For two miles we kept well up the hillside, and then descended at Cladach a' Ghlinne. We now turned farther inland and climbed to the summit of Ben Cleat. From there, at eight o'clock, we had just about the grandest view of all. The mist had lifted. Never had the Cuillin looked so stupendous. Every spire and pinnacle, every crag and splintered peak —and all of naked black rock—stood out clearly. Above us towered the shattered summit of Blaven, and beyond, the conical Red Hills were glistening in the dying glory of the sun.   Southwards was an archipelago of green islands: Canna, Eigg and the mountainous Rum, with, farther away, Ardnamurchan Point and the outlines of Tiree and Coll. Westwards were the peaks of Harris and North and South Uist, and to the east the rugged peninsula of Sleat separated us from the mainland.

It was nine o'clock when we straggled down to Elgol, to find the post-office closed. But when we pleaded " His Majesty's Service " the door was opened, the till unlocked, and we had our choice of postcards, peppermints and black striped balls. Then we trudged shorewards, and the Red One's persuasive tongue prevailed on an old dame to give us lodging. She was not keen on having us, as she was cleaning her kitchen and every stick of furniture was out on the front green. The fire was out! For once, and when we needed it most, no hot water or refreshing tea was forthcoming.

Supper was a dismal meal. The good woman was a worshipper of china: the mantelpiece, every press and shelf in her best room was crammed with cups, mugs and souvenir dishes of all descriptions, so that we were in constant dread of upsetting " A Present from Inverness," or breaking a Coronation plate. On the walls hung large, vividly coloured pictures from old magazines. A soldier, with a fierce moustache and side-whiskers, leaned over the hands of a long-skirted, wasp-waisted, balloon-sleeved damsel, while the caption below informed us that— " None but the Brave deserve the Fair." Just to show that no reflection on the senior service was intended there hung on the opposite wall a similar picture, but with a sailor instead of a soldier, the caption remaining the same. And, of course, Queen Victoria glared down on us disapprovingly.

Later we wandered down to the loch-side and bade good-bye to the mountains we had grown to love. It was a happy, peaceful scene, with old fishermen sitting smoking or yarning, a few boats on the glassy moonlit surface of Scavaig, and the harsh outline of the Cuillin softened by the grey hand of evening.

We knew something of Skye weather by now, and could predict with fair certainty a glorious day on the morrow. Nor were we disappointed; the discomfort of tramping on a road again was overcome by the enjoyment of that forenoon walk through lovely Strathaird. Blaven is such a mighty mountain that it seemed we would never get round him, but at last we got to the head of Loch Slapin, and lunched at the very spot where we had stopped a fortnight previously.

What a fortnight that had been! Then we were depressed by the wet weather; now we knew "every second day a wet one" to be a myth, for Skye had given us warm days and cool and beautiful evenings. Then we were having foot trouble; now we were bronzed, fit and thoroughly hardened. Then the mountains affected us "with astonishment"; now we knew something of their mighty peaks. Then we knew nothing of the kindly people; now we had new friends and hundreds of ineffaceable memories.

We tramped again by Torran and through Strath Suardal by the way we had come. Crofters were busy stacking peat for the winter; the bracken had grown higher, and on the little Loch of Cill Chriosd the water-lilies, in bud a fortnight ago, were in bloom. In the early afternoon we got to Broadford, slumbering under the shadow of Beinn na Caillich, and walked on—to Kyle—and home.

(For alternative routes see page 111.)

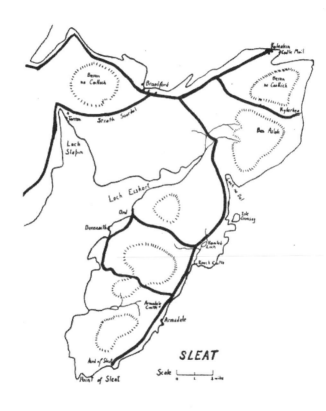

SLEAT

Kyleakin
Castle Maol

Beinn
na Caillich

Broadford

Beinn
na Caillich

Torrin

Kylerhea

Strath Suardal

Ben Aslak

Loch
Slapin

Loch Eishort

Kyle na Rea

Ord

Eilic
Donnan

Dunscaith

Knock
Loch

Knock Castle

Armadale Castle

Armadale

Aird of Sleat

Point of Sleat

Scale
0   1   2 miles

CHAPTER X

ALTERNATIVE ROUTES AND DISTANCES IN SKYE

1. KYLE OF LOCHALSH TO BROADFORD: 8 miles.
   See page 7.

2. KYLERHEA TO BROADFORD: 10 miles.

Kylerhea means " Straits of Rhea," Rhea being
a Fingalian warrior who once overestimated his
powers; he tried to jump across but fell in and was
drowned.

This is a hilly road through Glen Arroch, and
climbs to a height of over 800 feet. If fine, Beinn na
Caillich (2396) may be climbed. (This is the lower
of the two mountains of the same name in Skye.)
The old woman commemorated here was a giant
witch who spent her time throwing rocks at a sister
witch over in Raasay. So they say! It is a fine
viewpoint, both for the mainland hills and the Cuillin.
In making your plans, therefore, the qualification
should be added—"when the Cuillin are clear of
mist." While it is bright below, mist may hang over
the Cuillin for days at a time. So if you awake to
one of those heavenly Hebridean days which occur
now and then, forget all about your fixed itinerary
and do your climb that day. You may not get such
another during your holiday.

You will often be told of these lesser hills in Skye

which form good viewpoints, such as Ben Lee and
Meall a' Mhaim at Sligachan, and Fingal's Seat
and Ben Tianavaig at Portree.

The Kylerhea Beinn na Caillich can be climbed
almost directly from the pier, and the descent made
over Sgurr na Coinnich and down the western ridge
to the road. Taking in this hill, the distance to
Broadford would be about 14 miles.

3. Armadale to Broadford: 16 miles.

Travelling with a return ticket to Mallaig is the
cheapest way of reaching Skye, so many walkers
will start their journey from Armadale. The new
motor-boat ferry meets all trains, and does the
journey from Mallaig to Armadale in less than an
hour.

To one who has been in Skye previously, and
who has always travelled by Kyle of Lochalsh, the
most noticeable thing is the rich woodland around
Armadale, and this part of Sleat (pronounced *Slate*)
has been well named " The Garden of Skye."
Armadale itself is quite a small place, all the buildings being to the south of the pier. Buses connect
with the ferry to all parts of Skye. The tramper
for Broadford will turn north through the woods.
Armadale Castle, the modern residence of the
Macdonalds of the Isles, is hidden among the trees
on the west side of the road. Its situation—inland
instead of on a bold headland—dates it at once.
The Macdonalds deserted Duntulm about a hundred
years ago, and built this castle.

The road winds on, twisting and turning so that you never know what vista will open up next. Soon you will come to the parish church of Sleat, built near the site of one of the ancient duns or forts. On rising ground near by is the War Memorial to the " Men of Sleat." From here, ruins can be seen on the north side of Knock Bay. Leave the road a mile farther on and visit them. These walls are all that is left of what was once Castle Camas (Castle of the Bay), the stronghold of the Macdonalds of Sleat. Like the other old castles in Skye, its situation is superb.

There are many stories of this castle, particularly of one Mairi 'Chaisteil (Mary of the Castle), who once commanded it and withstood successfully the siege of the MacLeods. Of course the castle has its ghost, a wicked ghost this time, and said to be a she-devil in the shape of a grey goat.

The road now climbs up by Loch nan Dubhrachan (the Loch of the Black Braes). It is a pleasant little water-lily lochan. Appearances are often deceptive in Skye: this is the most notorious of all the haunted lochs on the island! A wicked water-horse dwelt therein, and terrorized the ancients. As recently as 1870 the loch was dragged. Suddenly the drag caught on something. With one accord the folks who had gathered to watch the operations turned and fled! For what could be obstructing the drag but the water-horse?

If you pass the kelpie safely you have a glorious tramp downhill to Isle Oronsay. It is a lovely

little village, and the bay, well sheltered by its
guardian island, is a favourite anchorage for small
craft.

Now you have a two-mile walk by Loch na Dal,
then leave the sea for a six-mile tramp over the
moors to Broadford Bay. There are no cottages by
the way, but half-way over is a spot where you may
wish to stop and linger. Not yet have I been able
to find the story about Drochaid Airidh na Suiridhe
(the Bridge of the Shieling of Courtship).

If it be evening the Red Hills will be aglow in
the setting sun. Let that be your beacon and guide
you to Broadford.

Via DUNSCAITH: 24 miles.

This is an alternative to going to Broadford the
first day. Spend the first evening at Armadale
(Point of Sleat could be visited in the afternoon)
and visit Dunscaith the next day. If this does not
leave you time to walk to Broadford that same day
you could join the evening bus which leaves Armadale
about 6 P.M. You leave the Broadford road two
miles north of Armadale pier and turn westwards.
As you tramp over the moor the Cuillin will come
into view beyond Strathaird. The road touches
Loch Eishort at Tarskavaig Bay and turns north to
Tokovaig.

You leave the road now and walk down to the
headland on the north shore of the bay. Little
remains now, but here once stood Dunscaith, the
Dunscaith of Ossian. Like Duntulm and Camas it

is on a crag by the sea, but with the added attraction of a background of the Cuillin Mountains.

If you would appreciate Dunscaith you must know something of its legends.

Its story goes back to the dim and distant past, when, they say, it was raised up by fairies in a single night. It became the stronghold of Queen Sguthach the Terrible, a great warrior who had a bodyguard of fivescore Amazons. Once when the Vikings raided the castle these women-warriors captured twenty of them, whom they promptly strung up by their long hair to the branches of trees, leaving them to sway in the wind till they died.

Then Cuchullain the Brave came out of Ireland. The story of how he got that name is worth the telling. His original name was Setanta and, even when a boy, he was famed for his great strength. Once he attended a banquet at the house of a noble called Culann. Suddenly Culann's favourite dog rushed at the boy. Setanta seized the dog by its hind-legs, dashed it against a wall and killed it. Whereupon there was a great outcry, and Culann threatened Setanta with death, because there was no other hound so good at guarding his dwelling. Setanta got out of the scrape by offering to guard the house himself till another dog was trained to take the dead hound's place. So he was called Cuchullain, which means " Culann's hound."

Well, Cuchullain came to Dunscaith to learn the art of war under Queen Sguthach. Many a time he took part in great deer-hunts all over the island, and there is a stone (Clach Luath) near the castle where, legend has it, he tied up his favourite hound, Luath, after the chase.

Cuchullain fell in love with Bragela, the beautiful daughter of Queen Sguthach. At last he had to return to the Irish wars and leave her behind. Ossian tells the story: " O strike the harp in praise of my love, the lonely sunbeam of Dunscaith! Strike the harp in praise of Bragela; she that I left in the Isle of Mist." Later, Cuchullain returned to Skye, and was killed in a fight while still a young man.

Many, many are the legends connecting Cuchullain with Dunscaith. The Cuillin Mountains are the dominating feature in the view from the castle, so many have claimed that the mountains are named after Ossian's hero, and that they should be called Cuchullain Mountains. Such great mountains would form a fitting memorial for such a mighty warrior.

Alas, the moderns will not have this interpretation, and say that the name is from A' Chuilionn (holly), from the resemblance of the ragged outline of the peaks to the edge of a holly leaf. At that rate Cuillin, the Ordnance Survey spelling, is wrong, the English equivalent of A' Chuilionn being Coolin.

Dunscaith was probably a stronghold of the Vikings for some time, and ultimately came into the possession of the Macdonalds. This was the first Skye castle of the Macdonalds, then they migrated to Duntulm and finally to Armadale. Yet all this was at a comparatively late period in the history of that clan, for the Macdonalds produce a genealogical tree which traces their descent to Breogan, twenty-third in descent from Japhet, son of Noah!

Anyway they were worthy successors to Queen Sguthach's warriors. Once a kinsman came to visit a certain chief. The chief's lady was entertaining twelve of *her* kinsmen. How he managed it the story does not say, but early one morning (probably when they were asleep) the chief's guest killed the other twelve and hung them up on a rope outside the lady's window, so that she would see them whenever she woke up. The chief does not appear to have objected and invited his kinsman to remain, but the murderer hurried off home, explaining that he did not think the chief's wife would be pleased!

Ord, two miles north of Dunscaith, is another place on this side of Sleat which will always be remembered. *A Summer in Skye* was the result of Alexander Smith's holiday with the McIains at their farm at Ord. Eighty years ago it was when he tramped these hills with Lachlan Roy and Angus-with-the-Dogs. It was from Ord he first saw Blaven, grew to love that mountain and composed the well-known poem.

In truth a road to linger over, and probably it will be late before you turn your back to the mountains and start the five-mile tramp across the moors to join the Broadford road again just near the haunted lochan.

4. The Red Hills.

These are the group of hills bounded by Strath Mòr, Strath Suardal and the road from Broadford to Loch Ainort. The climbing is nowhere difficult, though there is much tiring scree. The Broadford Beinn na Caillich is an even better viewpoint than the Kylerhea one. A round trip can be made by following the road as far as Strollamus, climbing Beinn na Caillich (2403) from the north, moving west to Beinn Dearg Mhòr (2323), east to Beinn Dearg Bheag, dropping down to Coirechatachan and so back to Broadford. The Skye rocks are magnetic, so that you cannot be sure of compass-readings. If the mist comes down you may very easily lose all sense of direction on these hills, but if you descend below the mist the landscape will show you your position. Quite possibly you will be on the wrong side of your hill!

5. Broadford to Sligachan.

Via Torran and Strath Mòr: 20 miles. See
     page 7.
Via Main Road: 18 miles.

From a motoring point of view this is one of the best stretches of road in Skye. Fortunately there are old roads left for the walker which will rejoice his heart. It is seldom that old roads are shorter than the new, but by taking to the old hill roads here the distance can be cut down to 15 miles. Take the main road to Strollamus and the old road across the point to Luib. From here you will see the new

motor road scarring the hillside on the opposite
shore of Loch Ainort. You need not go near it.
Take that delightful road from Kinloch Ainort over
Druim nan Cleochd to Sconser.

6. Sligachan to Coruisk and back by Camasunary:
   22 miles—very rough paths.

There is no walk quite like this in all Scotland
—through the wildest glen to the darkest loch. An
early start is essential; it is rough, hard going all
the time, and Glen Sligachan is not a place to
travel through in the dark. There is no spot by the
way where you may spend the night. It is truly a
terrible path, very stony, and often in the nature
of a mud-bath.

From the inn cross the bridge, and take the path
up the east side of the river. As you get deeper
and deeper into the glen, with the black crags on
either side, you will understand the meaning of
utter desolation. About four miles out you will at
last get round Sgurr nan Gillean and see up into
Harta Corrie, where once a clan battle was fought.
A short way beyond this you will pass two little
lochans (the Black Lochans). Beyond the lochans
the path forks, to the left for Camasunary and
to the right for Coruisk. You may lose the path
about here, but if you continue south and make
for the top of the Drumhain ridge (1000 feet) you
should be able to pick it up somewhere.

Some may not feel inclined to go farther, and will
return to Sligachan from Drumhain (about 13 miles

altogether). The ridge is a grand viewpoint, with the walls of Blaven to the west and all the Cuillin crags circling round to the east, but does not give a proper view of Coruisk.

From the ridge the path continues down towards Loch Scavaig to what is known as the viewpoint, and it is worth while going as far as this. To get to the shore of Coruisk you leave the path a little before this and climb down near the Allt Choire Riabhaich. You can then walk to where the River Scavaig leaves the loch, from where you will find a well-marked path to Port Sgaile. Don't let the name delude you: there are no buildings—only a landing-place on the rocks.

The route from here to Camasunary has already been described (page 84).

From Camasunary the path winds up past the west side of Loch na Creitheach and Loch an Athain to join the outward path near the Dubh Lochans.

Sir Walter Scott, in his journal, tells how his party landed in the wrong bay and walked to Loch na Creitheach thinking it was Loch Coruisk.

If you wish to make a one-way journey you may continue from Camasunary to Elgol (see page 87), the total distance being about 15 miles.

There is also a path for three miles across the hills from Camasunary to join the Elgol-Broadford road at Kilmarie. It is well marked by cairns. Beyond the highest point take the path which leads to the south; the other goes into private ground in the vicinity of Strathaird House.

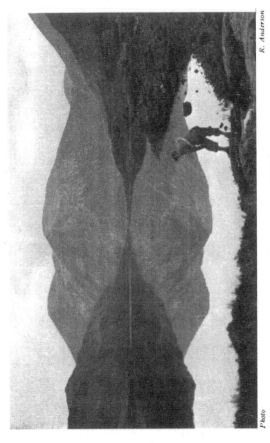

Photo

R. *Anderson*

ON THE ROAD TO CAMASUNARY

Marsco and Rhinadh Star reflected in Loch na Creitheach

[Facing page 100

A. E. Robertson

THE BLOODY STONE—HARTA CORRIE

7. SLIGACHAN.

The Red Cuillin.—These are the group of hills to
the east of Glen Sligachan, and comprise Glamaig
(2537), Beinn Dearg (2389) and Marsco (2411).
The climbing is much the same as on Beinn na
Caillich.   Glamaig is the nearest mountain to
Sligachan, and is well worth ascending.   A circuit
can be made by climbing from the north-east from
somewhere near Sconser Lodge.   This is the easiest
route and avoids almost all the scree.   You will
strike a deer-fence which will lead you to the summit,
and which is a useful direction-finder should you
be caught in the mist.   The descent can be made to
the col (Bealach na Sgairde) between Glamaig and
Beinn Dearg and so back to Sligachan, or, if feeling
energetic, you may continue and climb Beinn Dearg,
going as far as Beinn Dearg Mheadhonach and
descending by its western ridge.

You will probably be told of General Bruce's
Gurkha soldier, who, starting from Sligachan Bridge,
climbed Glamaig and returned to the bridge within
an hour.   Do not estimate your time from his!
You will probably take an hour and a half to two
hours for the ascent alone.

The Round Hill.—Meall a' Mhaim (1335) is the
small hill just to the north of the Bealach a' Mhaim.
It is a splendid viewpoint on a good day.

The Cuillin Corries.—The tramper should try to
visit at least one of the greater corries.   The Bloody
Stone in Harta Corrie, which is said to mark the

spot of a great clan fight, is about a mile up the corrie from the Sligachan-Coruisk path. Don't try to go direct from there to the north end of Coruisk, return and make for the Drumhain ridge.

Coire na Creiche (Corrie of the Spoil).—This was also the site of a clan fight, between the MacLeods and the Macdonalds. Leave the Sligachan-Loch Brittle path just beyond the summit of the pass and turn left round Bruach na Frithe into the corrie. There is, of course, no path and the going, as in all Cuillin corries, is terribly rough.

If energetic you can continue farther into the corrie where it divides into Coir a' Mhadaidh and Coire Tairneilear (Corrie of the Thunderer). The crag jutting out between these is Sgurr an Fheadain (the Peak of the Chanter). The famous water-pipe gully is on this crag, and the start of the climb could be visited.

Coire Lagan and Coir' a' Ghrundha have already been mentioned, and their lonely lochans make them specially interesting. These are too far away to be visited in a one-day excursion from Sligachan, but are easily accessible from Loch Brittle.

8. SLIGACHAN TO LOCH BRITTLE.

Via ROAD: 14 miles.

Take the Dunvegan road as far as Drynoch Bridge (5 miles), walk along the south shore of Loch Harport and turn south by the road which leads from Carbost to Loch Brittle. For those who prefer rough hill paths to motor roads there is a better route over the Bealach a' Mhaim (the Pass of the Round Hill).

Via BEALACH A' MHAIM: 5 miles rough path; 4 miles road.

The path leaves the Dunvegan road about a quarter of a mile from the inn and crosses the moor to a deserted cottage near the Allt Dearg Mòr. The route to Sgurr nan Gillean crosses the burn here, but the Loch Brittle route continues on its northern side. As you climb up you have a fine view of the pinnacle ridge of Sgurr nan Gillean. The path keeps well above the burn, which tumbles down by a series of waterfalls. Several cairns mark the route and a large one the summit of the pass.

From the Bealach you will see the road from Carbost winding over the moor, and the path leads down to join it just where it turns into Glen Brittle. Now you have a four-mile walk to the loch-side past two fine corries, Coire Ghreadaidh and Coire na Banachdich.

9. SLIGACHAN TO PORTREE.

Via MAIN ROAD: 9 miles. See page 21.
Via BEN LEE: 4 miles hills; 8 miles road.

If the day be fine this is much the better route for the walker. Just beyond the inn on the Portree road turn to the right, and move down to the Sligachan river. A path leads along the loch-side to Peinchorran. Follow this for about a mile, and take to the hills just beyond Allt an t-Sithein (the Fairies' Burn). Ben Lee is only 1456 feet high and

the going is easy all the way. From here make your
way down to the north-east, joining the road from
Peinchorran to Portree at the hamlet of Ollach. Now
continue north to Tianavaig Bay and cross the moor to
join the main road about three miles south of Portree.

If you seek the " wee folk " then you will descend
farther south, for the Braes district was a favourite
haunt of the Skye fairies in the olden days.

10. PORTREE—FINGAL'S SEAT—BEN TIANAVAIG—
THE STORR.

All are good viewpoints on clear days. The route to
Fingal's Seat (see page 27) is up by the golf course.

Ben Tianavaig (1352) is perhaps a better viewpoint, with the added attraction of splendid cliffs
on the seaward side. Leave the Portree-Peinchorran
road about half-way between Peinmore House and
Tianavaig Bay and climb up from the south-west.
The return journey will be about 10 miles.

The Storr (2360) is a much stiffer climb than
either of the other two. Leave the road between
Loch Fada and Loch Leatham, about four miles
north of Portree, and climb to the ridge at Bealach
Mòr, or five miles out and climb up to Bealach
Beag. Either way the return journey will be about
15 miles. There is much rock to the east, and the
hill should be avoided on a misty day.

11. PORTREE TO STAFFIN.
Via HILL-TOPS.   See page 31.

It is difficult to estimate the distance here, but
it must be at least 24 miles of hill-walking, probably

more. This is a journey only for the strongest walkers, and can be done only on a really good day. An early start is essential. Keep to the road if there is any hint of mist.

Via ROAD: 17 miles.

This is a post-War road but looks much older. As you top the road about three miles north of Portree you have splendid views of the Cuillin to the south and the Storr to the north. You descend now and pass Loch Fada, where once dwelt a water-kelpie, and on to Loch Leatham. Both these lochs are famous for their trout. Beyond Loch Leatham you may leave the road and visit the Old Man of Storr, a crazy pinnacle, 150 feet high, like the Needle Rock at the Quiraing. There are also other pinnacles, and the whole rock formation is on a weird and fantastic scale.

Returning to the road you continue uphill and down dale to Rigg (9 miles out) and the River Lealt (11 miles out). The gorge is worth a visit. A path leads from the bridge down the south side of the river to a sheltered little bay. When the river is low you can cross to the north side, visit the remains of the diatomite-works and return to the road by the zigzag track which was once a light railway. From the road you will see the track leading up into the hills. Many of the sleepers remain, but are so grown over with grass as to be hardly distinguishable. Diatomite is a substance found at the bottom of fresh-water lochs in certain localities, which, after treatment, has several industrial uses. It is a non-conductor of heat, and when mixed with cement was used for fireproof walls, etc. Scientific methods of manufacture in Germany killed the business, but before it was abandoned, some years ago, the diatomite was dug up from a little loch (Loch Cuithir) in the hills, which had been drained and then dried, conveyed by the light railway to the sheds at the shore-side for treatment and shipped to the mainland.

From the River Lealt the road climbs again, past the little village of Culnacnock (13 miles out), to Loch Mealt.

Only the road divides the loch from the top of the cliffs, and if you walk over to them just south of the waterfall you have a view both of the waterfall and the Kilt Rock, half-a-mile to the north. What remains of Dun Greanan (the Sunny Fort), on the north shore of Loch Mealt, should also be visited. The road turns inland now till it reaches Staffin Bay, one of the prettiest bays in the Isle of Mist. If you visit the Old Man of Storr and the diatomite-works the distance will be about 20 miles.

12. Staffin to Uig: *via* Flodigarry and Duntulm: 14 miles. See page 38.

Across the Island: 8 miles.

There is not a single building the whole way across the moor. There are short cuts at the hairpin bends at the summit of the road and when going down to Uig. To visit the Quiraing, leave the road

about two miles out of Staffin and pick up the path
which leads up by the Needle Rock. When returning, bear farther to the west and join the road
near its highest point.

13. UIG TO DUNVEGAN: 29 miles. See page 43.

This journey can be cut down to 23 miles if you
take the ferry from Romesdal to Treaslane. There
is a notice by the roadside just before you come to
the bridge over the River Romesdal, and a road
leads down to a cottage beside an old mill. Probably Edinbain, 20 miles for Dunvegan (14 using
ferry), will be far enough for one day.

14. DUNVEGAN TO CLAIGAN: 4½ miles.

Most people visiting Dunvegan Castle do not go
beyond it. A pleasant road leads on to the north-
west and gives good views of the many islands on
the loch and the fine position of the castle. About
a mile beyond it an attempt has been made to
transform an inlet of the sea into a fresh-water
loch. There is a ford here, but the walker can
continue along the embankment. You may leave
the road and turn west over to the headland, where
there are ruins of an ancient fort rather better
preserved than usual. The road now keeps farther
inland, till it finishes at Claigan. The return journey
is made by the same route.

15. DUNVEGAN TO GLENDALE: 8 miles; to NEIST
    POINT: 11 miles. See page 52.

If you do not wish to go and return by same
route then climb Healaval More first, descend to

north-west, and you will strike a path which leads down the east side of the River Hamra to Glendale.

16. DUNVEGAN TO BORERAIG : 7 miles; to DUNVEGAN HEAD : 10 miles.

Take the Glendale road to Colbost. Continue by the loch-side instead of climbing the hill, pass through Husabost to Boreraig. Sheriff Nicolson, the Skye poet, was born at Husabost. At Boreraig a hollow between the road and the shore is pointed out as the site of the famous piping school of the Macrimmons. Dunvegan Head is three miles farther on, but, of the two headlands, Neist Point is the more interesting.

17. DUNVEGAN.

MacLeod's Tables. — Healaval More (1538) and Healaval Beg (1601) are the proper names of these two flat-topped hills which are such conspicuous features of the landscape in this part of Skye. Both may be easily climbed in one day, starting at Dunvegan and coming down at Orbost. The climbing is easy, but there is much very marshy ground. If only one is to be climbed then a personal opinion is that Healaval Beg is the better viewpoint, and is best reached by Glen Osdale.

The Caves.—The pipers' cave at Harlosh Point can be visited by road (see page 61). A good plan if there is a party is to hire a motor-boat, with which you can visit the caves at Orbost Point, at Harlosh Point, and MacLeod's Maidens at Idrigill Point. You can also go to Neist Point by motor-boat. You will see a notice advertising the boat at Roskill where the road leads down to the Vatten Peninsula, and particulars may also be obtained in Dunvegan.

18. DUNVEGAN TO CARBOST: 20 miles. See page 60.

When the tide is out it is possible to take a short cut across the end of Loch Beag, and also to cross the River Drynoch instead of continuing to the bridge.

19. DUNVEGAN TO SLIGACHAN: 22 miles.

20. DUNVEGAN TO PORTREE.

The tramper returning to Portree from Dunvegan has the choice of two routes: either north by the Fairy Bridge and Loch Snizort, or south to Bracadale, then across the moors. The distance in either case is about 23 miles. From Bracadale a road winds over the moors and there is no shelter the whole long length of it. It is not a motor road, so should have the walker's preference.

21. CARBOST TO FISKAVAIG AND TALISKER AND BACK TO CARBOST: 12 miles.

There is a road as far as Fernilea, where a path leads up to the left and over the moor to Fiskavaig Bay. From here another path crosses over between two hills to Talisker. From Talisker there is a road up by the River Talisker and back to Carbost, a road which Samuel Johnson and his party travelled over. Note that the famous Talisker Distillery is at Carbost, and not at Talisker!

In that fine book *The Key above the Door* Maurice Walsh makes Tom King do an interesting day's tramp from Carbost, and the route is worth following.

From Uiskavagh (Carbost) he followed the road to Loch Brittle. Then, in his own words: " I crossed the high shoulder of Bein Breinish and came down on that deep and dark Loch Chroisg, edged round that sullen water and faced the brae beyond. Over the head of that brae I dipped into the gentle valley of Loch Sleadale, where the good brown trout lurk, and are not shy of the fisherman's lure." You will not find these names on the map. The route would be from Loch Brittle over Bealach Brittle to Loch Eynort (Loch Chroisg), round the head of that loch and over the hills to Loch Sleadale, then to Talisker and by road to Carbost. About 25 miles it will be, and half of it on the hills.

In passing, though it is out of place here, the same book describes a grand walk from " Loch Ruighi in the Province of Moray " to Achnasheen which would form a fitting " Road to the Isles."

22. CARBOST TO LOCH BRITTLE.

Via ROAD: 9 miles. See route 8.

Via LOCH EYNORT: 4 miles road; 5 miles moorland. See page 71.

23. LOCH BRITTLE TO RUDH' AN DUNAIN: 4 miles moorland.

The tramper and camper at Loch Brittle should not omit to visit this point (Point of the Little Fort).

The ancient dun is fairly well marked, not far from Lochan na h'Airde (Lochan of the Point).   This was once a stronghold of the MacAskalls, adherents of the MacLeods, who acted as coastguards against the raids of the Macdonalds.

24. LOCH BRITTLE TO CORUISK: 8 miles; to CAMASUNARY: 11 miles; to ELGOL: 16 miles. No path Loch Brittle to Coruisk; rough path Coruisk to Elgol.   See page 81.

This is rather a strenuous journey, especially with a heavy pack.   Once committed to it you must continue, there is no place by the way where you can rest for the night.   From Coruisk you may return to Sligachan instead of going on to Elgol. From Coruisk allow about three and a half hours to Loch Brittle, Sligachan or Elgol.

25. ELGOL TO BROADFORD: 14 miles; to KYLE OF LOCHALSH: 22 miles.   See page 88.

CHAPTER XI

Lone places of the deer,
  Corrie and loch and ben,
Fount that wells in the cave,
  Voice of the burn and wave,
Softly you sing and clear
  Of Charlie and his men!

Here has he lurked, and here
  The heather has been his bed,
The wastes of the island ken
  And the Highland hearts were true
To the bonnie, the brave, the dear,
  The royal, the hunted head.

AYTOUN.

HAD Prince Charlie been able to sail direct to France after the disaster at Culloden it is very questionable if, in song and story, he would be remembered with such affection to-day. It is characteristic of the Highlanders that Charlie as a poor outlaw was more loved and better served than as a victorious commander. The story of his later years on the Continent is a sad one, and there can be little doubt that his five months' wandering in the Highlands and Islands was one of the happiest periods in his life.

The Prince surely was a trampers' hero: a strong hillman, who could tramp the long day over the roughest country, who could find a night's rest on the heather, who thought nothing of a thorough soaking, and who could at all times keep cheery and good-humoured.

And what can we say of Flora Macdonald, who was under no obligation to act as his guide, but who "joyfully accepted the offer without the least hesitation"? The Prince remained in Skye for six days; for three days only Flora was his guide, yet but for these three days the island's story—aye, the story of Scotland—would be immeasurably the poorer.

The battle of Culloden was fought on 16th April 1746. After many adventures the Prince gained the coast, and sailed to the Outer Hebrides, about a fortnight later. Then came fugitive trips from island to island, cold and wet nights in caves and among the heather, the while soldiers hunted for him by land and sloops-of-war by sea. The pursuit became too close, and it was decided he should go to Skye dressed as Flora Macdonald's serving-maid.

Late at night on the 28th June a six-oared boat— the best boat in all the Lews—set out from South Uist and crossed the Minch to Skye. A wild, stormy night it was, but the Blue Men of the Minch were on their side and saw them safely over They touched the island at Vaternish Point, but soldiers were camping there and they could not land. They then crossed Loch Snizort, and finally landed at Kilbride Point, about half-a-mile south of Monkstadt House. Flora went up to seek the aid of her kins-woman, Lady Macdonald, only to find that soldiers searching for the Prince were camping near by, while their captain was actually in the house. Nothing daunted, she engaged him in conversation, and allayed his suspicions when he queried about the Prince.

In the late afternoon the party set off for Kingsburgh. Militia were stationed at Uig, so even bridle-paths had to be avoided at times. It is not possible to trace the exact route—it would probably be to the west of the present road. Many detours must have been made, as the distance by road is less than fifteen miles, and the party did not arrive at Kingsburgh till midnight. The Prince's disguise was very poor, and villagers who saw him had a good idea of his identity. He must in truth have been a queer figure in petticoats. Kingsburgh's daughter ran upstairs to tell her mother that her father had brought home " a most muckle ill-shapen wife," and the good lady herself described him as " an odd muckle trallup of a carline."

At Kingsburgh the Prince slept in a bed—the only time he had such comfort in Skye—and slept soundly till the next afternoon. It was here that Flora cut off that lock of his hair now jealously preserved at Dunvegan. Flora also took one of the sheets from the bed in which he slept, kept it through-out her life, and it now lies with her in the kirkyard at Kilmuir. The house the Prince stayed at is now a ruin, the present building being more modern.

After leaving Kingsburgh the Prince tired of woman's clothing and changed into his old ragged kilt before continuing on the road to Portree. His route would be in the direction of the present road. It rained heavily, and the Prince arrived at the inn (the predecessor of the Royal Hotel) thoroughly soaked. The island of Raasay was the objective of his guides, but as there were soldiers stationed in the village they did not dare arouse suspicion by using one of the Portree boats. Two followers of the Laird of Raasay went to Loch Fada, three miles to the north, carried and dragged a boat from there to the coast and brought it to Portree. One has only to walk from Loch Fada to the cliffs to appreciate what a difficult job this must have been. These freshwater-loch boats are usually small, old and unseaworthy; such was the boat that carried a prince to Raasay.

He rested there for a day, then returned to Skye, landing north of Portree, and spending the night in a byre at Scorrybreck. This has disappeared, and is not marked on the half-inch map. It was situated near the ancient Dun Torvaig, about three-quarters of a mile north-east of Portree.

Then began Charlie's most strenuous journey in Skye. With one guide (a MacLeod) he walked from Scorrybreck to Elgol. The guide must have been very sure of the Prince's ability as a hillman when they did not start this journey till six o'clock at night. The modern tramper would want a full day, and few would care to undertake this journey overnight. No description of the exact route is available and the route given here is made up from the various accounts of the Prince's wanderings in Skye.

From Scorrybreck they circled round Portree and tramped southwards, keeping to the west of the present road and to the west of the River Varragill. We are told that soldiers were camping at Sligachan, so they would keep well inland. It might have been somewhere about Loch na Caiplaich that the Prince was bogged up to the waist and had to be pulled out by MacLeod. They crossed the Red Burn, the moor behind the present inn, and the River Sligachan farther up the glen.

Some writers say that they continued up Glen Sligachan, through Strath na Creitheach to Cama-sunary, and by the coast to Elgol. This is certainly the obvious route to Strathaird, but it does not explain why Strath Mòr has been associated with the Prince. We like to think he took this other route— and it is probable that he did so—for it makes him climb a Skye mountain. It would make them climb up to the col between Marsco and Beinn Dearg, descend to the corrie at the head of Loch Ainort, and circle round Glas Bheinn Mhòr into Strath Mòr.

Their route from the head of Loch Slapin would be in the direction of the present road from Torran to Elgol. A midsummer night in Skye is very short, but for three hours at least of their journey they must have travelled in darkness. It is little wonder that Charlie, in darkness, in the heart of the mountains, exclaimed: " I'm sure the Devil could not find me now!"

In the morning of 4th July they entered the house of one Mackinnon, and had breakfast there. They must have been well ready for a meal, as we are told they carried no provisions with them. They were later—for it was thought unsafe for them to remain in the house—directed to a cave on the shore, on the opposite side of Strathaird from the Spar Cave. Here the Prince remained till evening, and was then rowed over to Mallaig.

His troubles were not over. He had another two-and-a-half-months wanderings in the West Highlands before he was able to join a ship for France. Time and time again he was near capture. Always there were good friends to help. Surely no prince has ever commanded such loyalty! There was a reward of £30,000 for his capture. He met hundreds of Highlanders to whom this sum was wealth untold, but never was there any hint of betrayal. Fittingly does Aytoun make Charlie say in his later years in France:

> " Give me back my trusty comrades!
>   Give me back my Highland maid!
> Nowhere beats the heart so kindly
>   As beneath the tartan plaid! "

SAMUEL JOHNSON'S ROUTE IN SKYE

Johnson and Boswell may be regarded as the first of all English tourists. They visited Skye in September 1773, only twenty-seven years after the '45 Rebellion, and spent a month on the island. Perhaps it was they who founded the tradition, which still exists in the South, that August and September are the best months for holidaying in the Highlands, though we in the North know that May and June are the better months.

Johnson's party experienced very bad weather, his journal tells again and again of delays owing to rain. Beinn na Caillich is the only mountain he mentions, probably because the legend of the Norse Princess interested him. To us it seems amazing that he should have passed by Sligachan, through Glen Drynoch, and visited Carbost and Talisker, without the Black Cuillin Mountains making the slightest impression on him. We will be charitable and assume that, in the wet weather Johnson experienced in Skye, the Cuillin were hidden in the mist most of the time.

Life was unhurried in those days; the party travelled slowly, by easy stages, and spent a few days at each of the houses they visited. During these halts they do not appear to have explored the neighbouring countryside, but spent their time in talking, and talk, after all, was Johnson's chief joy in life.

Again we must remember that, at that time, there

were no proper roads in Skye. This explains why the party so frequently travelled by sea. One has only to tramp over the present hill paths in Skye to understand how uncomfortable and tedious the journeying must have been to a stout and querulous old man mounted on a shaggy hill pony. It is not surprising that he was at times ill-humoured.

Johnson and Boswell left Glenelg on 2nd September, and were rowed down the Sound of Sleat to Armadale. It rained most of the time and they discovered, as all visitors to the island discover sooner or later, that Skye rain is very wetting. At this date Armadale Castle had not been built, so they were entertained by Sir Alexander Macdonald at a tenant's house. The Macdonald was not the island chief of Johnson's imagination and he, rather tactlessly for a guest, tried to point out his deficiencies to him. The atmosphere at times appears to have been rather strained.

From Armadale they rode past Isle Oronsay, over the moor and through Broadford to the house of one Mackinnon, at Coirechatachan. The route would probably be much the same as the present road (route 3, page 92). Of the journey Johnson says only that it occupied a whole day: "from Armidale we came at night to Coire Chatachan." This is noticeable through the journal: Johnson has surprisingly little to say about the actual journeying from place to place; he was mainly concerned with collecting information about the habits and customs of the islanders.

At Coirechatachan occurred Johnson's nearest approach to mountaineering—" the hill behind the house we did not climb "—implying almost that they could have climbed it had they desired. Imagination cannot stretch to Johnson labouring up the steep scree slopes of Beinn na Caillich.

A day was spent at Coirechatachan, then the party rode two miles to the coast at Sgianadan, and from there crossed over to Raasay. During their three days on the island the visitors do not appear to have walked far from the laird's house.

From Raasay they went by boat to Portree, and rode on ponies, and in rain, to Kingsburgh, again probably taking the path of the present road. The Laird of Kingsburgh of this time was the husband of the same Flora Macdonald who journeyed with Prince Charlie twenty-seven years previously. Johnson describes her as " a woman of middle stature, soft features, gentle manners and elegant presence."

From her own lips Johnson heard the story of the Prince's wanderings, and actually slept in the same bed as Charlie had used. Even he, the hard-headed critic, perceived something of the romance. His own journey may be forgotten, but never the words in which he prophesied truly of Flora: " a name that will be mentioned in history and, if courage and fidelity be virtue, mentioned with honour."

After a day at Kingsburgh they crossed Loch Snizort to Greshornish and travelled to Dunvegan Castle, the latter part of the route being by the road already described. They stayed at Dunvegan for nine days, where they enjoyed themselves immensely. The lairds they met there were called after their places of residence, with the exception of an island gentleman who objected to being known as Muck!

Other than exploring the castle most thoroughly, and visiting Rory Mòr's waterfall when the burn was in spate, the visitors appear to have spent most of their time indoors. The present trees around the castle have grown up within the last hundred years, so that the whole place would seem much bleaker than nowadays.

From Dunvegan they travelled to Ullinish, two miles west of Bracadale, and, from there, visited, by boat, the Piper's Cave at Harlosh Point.

Those who know the virtue of black and strong Skye tea will have a fellow-feeling for the old man. While at Ullinish they say he consumed twenty-two cups of it! This must surely have been in the course of the two days he remained there. Even Johnson would find it difficult to drink twenty-two cups of tea at one meal.

Once more they took a short cut by sea, from Ullinish across Loch Harport to Fernilea, whence they rode on ponies to Talisker, following the path of the present road up the Carbost Burn across the moor and down Glen Talisker to the sea. Here Boswell seems to have been mighty pleased with himself because he climbed " Prieshwell." The present map shows Preshal More and Preshal Beg. The former, about 1000 feet high, is nearer Talisker, and is probably the one Boswell climbed.

From Talisker they rode through Glen Drynoch to the inn at Sconser. There is no inn at the present village of Sconser, and that visited by Johnson was on the site of Sconser Lodge. That inn was also the meeting-place where the Skye chiefs refused to support Prince Charlie's cause in '45.

At Sconser the guides decided that the ponies were not capable of carrying the bulky Englishman over Druim nan Cleochd. Knowing that terrible road one is not surprised. They made a much quicker journey by boat, landed at Strollamus, four miles north of Broadford, and returned to the hospitable roof of Coirechatachan.

Here Johnson forgot, for once, that he was a famous scholar and took a lively part in what we would now call a real cheery night.

They then rode southwards by the way they had come, to Ostaig in Sleat, where they were detained for three days by bad weather " at the margin of the sea," and finally left Skye on the 3rd of October.

To the motorist of to-day who runs round Skye in an afternoon Johnson's may not seem much of a journey. But let him hire a hill pony and follow faithfully Johnson's route *without ever going over a modern road*. He will then change his opinion, and appreciate the old man's powers as a traveller.

CHAPTER XII

But in the prime of summer-time,
Give me the Isle of Skye!

NICOLSON.

THE walking tour described in the main part of this book was carried out several years ago, and it is a very suitable route for a first visit. Omitting the high-level route from the Storr to the Quiraing it has the merit of leaving the roughest country to the last, when you should be thoroughly fit. On subsequent visits, when the other routes were covered, it was impossible to recapture the glamour of that first tramp round the island, but the old charm remained; that is undying. I envy the tramper who has yet to see Blaven burst into view at that bend on the Strathaird road, who has yet to witness his first Skye sunset, who has yet to climb his first Skye mountain and behold the Hebrides.

A close study of the map will suggest infinite variations, but to keep rigidly to a previously fixed itinerary is to spoil your holiday; rather decide each morning—according to the weather and the state of your feet—just how little or how much you are going to do. Don't attempt to cover too much ground: return again the following year. It will take many holidays to exhaust the charms of Skye.

Skye caters for every class of tramper. The walker who wishes to keep to good roads can go round the island and never be far away from a motor road, and, let me whisper it, can join a bus when the flesh is weak. The walker who prefers to avoid the motor roads can still go round the island and travel on them only for a few miles.

His route would be: Armadale to Broadford *via* Dunscaith, Broadford to Sligachan by Strath Mòr and the old hill roads, Sligachan to Portree *via* Peinchorran or Ben Lee, Portree to Staffin *via* the Storr, Staffin to Uig *via* Quiraing, Uig to Skeabost (main road) across country to Edinbain, path from Edinbain across Vaternish to Lusta, Lusta to Dunvegan, Dunvegan to Carbost (main road)—then he has the choice of all the country between Drynoch and Strathaird, where there are hardly any roads at all.

The walker with less time could either avoid Sleat, by taking bus or boat to Broadford or Portree, or avoid Trotternish, by taking the moorland road from Portree to Bracadale and Dunvegan.

The walker who is interested in "old unhappy far-off things" will find much to his liking in Skye: stone circles, relics of pagan rites in the distant past; ruins of forts built by the early Celts to keep out the Viking raiders, and castles built by the clan chiefs.

Little remains of the stone circles. The best-marked one is just at the roadside at the top of the hill south of Uig.

It would take several holidays in Skye before one could visit all the old forts (duns). There are about fifty of them marked on the map, for the most part round the coastline, and a visit to them all would mean a journey of several hundred miles. The sites of some of them are well marked, of others a heap of stones remain, while of many the position is indicated only by a grassy mound.

Dun also means a little hill, so perhaps some were never really forts at all. There is not, as might be expected, a regular chain of forts round the island; rather are they in groups, with the individual forts of each group within easy distance of each other. Usually the situation is on a slight eminence, so that warning signals could be passed from fort to fort.

The position of the groups indicates the populated parts of the island in the older days.

Going round the coast from Kyleakin the duns are:

East Coast:

Dun an Aird: on a point north-east of Peinchorran.

Dun Torvaig: about half-a-mile north-east of Portree.

Dun Borve (1): on the hillside to east of clachan of Borve (Portree-Skeabost road).

Dun Dugan: on a hill two miles north of Portree.

Dun Gernshader: to the east of the Portree-Staffin road, one mile north of Portree.

Dun Greanan (1): on coast to south of River Lealt.

Dun Connabern: on the moor to west of village of Culnacnock.

Dun Raisaburgh: to the south of Loch Mealt.

Dun Greanan (2): on north shore of Loch Mealt.

Dun Mòr: on hillside to east of Quiraing.

Dun Vallerain: near Loch Vallerain, two miles north of Staffin.

Dun Vannerain: a mile north of Kilmaluag.

West Coast :

Dun Liath: on a point two miles north of Monkstadt.

Dun Skudiburg: on a point two miles south of Monkstadt.

Dun Eyre: on a hill half-a-mile to east of Romesdal Bridge.

Dun Suledale: on the moor between Bernisdale and Edinbain near Clachanish.

Dun (unnamed): on the hillside east of Edinbain.

Dun Flashader: on the east shore of Loch Greshornish.

Dun Borve (2): a mile south of Dun Flashader.

Dun Cearymore: near Vaternish Point.

Dun Borrafiach: a mile south of Dun Cearymore.

Dun Hallin: Vaternish, on hill east of Hallin.

Dun (unnamed): on a peninsula north of Dunvegan.

Dun Colbost: west of Colbost (Dunvegan-Glendale road).

Dun Boreraig (1): south of Boreraig.

Dun (unnamed): a mile north of Orbost.

Dun Elireach: Harlosh, west side of Vatten Peninsula.

Dun Neill: near Harlosh Point.

Dun Feorlig: east side of Vatten Peninsula.

Dun Arkaig: in Glen Ullinish, three miles east of
   Loch Caroy.

Dun Mòr (2) and Dun Beag (1): within half-a-mile of
   each other on the hillside north of Bracadale.

Dun Diarmaid: east shore of Loch Beag.

Dun Tungadal: head of Glen Bracadale, near Loch
   Duagrich.

Dun Taimh: to the west of main road two miles
   south of Bracadale.

Dun (unnamed): north shore of Fiskavaig Bay.

Dun (unnamed): south shore of Loch Eynort, west
   of Kraiknish.

Dun Grugaig: east side of Strathaird to south of
   Spar Cave.

Dun Ringill: on shore to east of Strathaird House.

Dun Mòr (3): west of Torran.

Dun Beag (2): south of Torran.

Dun Kearstach: west shore of Loch Slapin about a
   quarter of a mile inland.

Dun Boreraig (2): north shore of Loch Eishort.

Dun Geilht: west coast of Sleat near Caradal.

Dun Bàn: on shore to east of Aird of Sleat.

Dun a Cheleirich: about half-a-mile north of Dun
   Bàn.

Dun Chlo: about a mile north of Dun a Cheleirich.

Dun Faich: near Sleat Kirk.

Dun Bàn (2): on shore a mile south of Isle Oronsay.

Dun Ruaige: on shore a mile south of Kylerhea.

Quite probably you will content yourself with
exploring the ancient castles.   All five—Camas,

Moil, Dunscaith, Dunvegan and Duntulm—could easily be visited on one trip round the island. The last three, as their names imply, were built on the sites of earlier duns. A visit to Dunvegan should on no account be omitted. This castle is open to the public on Tuesday and Thursday afternoons, so you should arrange to be at Dunvegan on either of these days.

Map.—Generally the tramper arms himself with the Ordnance Survey one-inch-to-the-mile map. Unfortunately the part containing Skye is divided into four sections, so is unsuitable. Bartholomew's half-inch-to-the-mile map (Scotland, sheet 19) contains the whole island and the adjacent mainland, and bears every place-name mentioned in this book. It is quite satisfactory, though if you have previously used a one-inch map you are apt to underestimate the distance to be covered when using the half-inch one.

A compass cannot be relied on, as the Skye rocks are magnetic and affect the needle.

Kit.—Each tramper has his own ideas, and it is better for the beginner to learn by experience just what is essential and what is useless. The walker should be able to keep his pack down to about fifteen pounds; the camper's will be over twenty, and probably nearer thirty if he is going into the wilder parts of the island.

Boots are better than shoes if you intend to do much on the hills: unprotected ankles may be badly bruised on the scree slopes. Skye rain is *very* wetting,

THE STORR AND THE OLD MAN

Photo

W. J. MacArthur

[Facing page 129

ON THE ROCKS OF THE QUIRAING

and a change of clothing is welcome. It will also add much to your comfort if you take some reliable anti-midge lotion with you.

Climbing.—The Trotternish Hills, the Duirinish Hills, the Red Hills and the Red Cuillin offer ordinary hill-climbing, though there is much tiring scree among the two last-mentioned groups.

The Black Cuillin are mountains quite different from any other range in Scotland. Our mainland hills, though they may have rock faces, have usually an easy way up. This is not so with the Cuillin. These mountains are the cragsman's paradise, and many of them can be climbed only by the experienced rock climber.

The lone walker should keep clear of them altogether.

The tramper who wishes to experience the joy of rock-climbing should try to arrange with someone who knows the mountains to lead the way. There are no organized rock-climbing guides in Skye, as in Lakeland. John Mackenzie does not climb now, though it may be possible to get the services of another guide at Sligachan Inn.

Of the major peaks some may be climbed by novices, provided always they have a clear day, a good day for heights and a well-nailed pair of boots. The easiest is Bruach na Frithe, starting from about the summit of Bealach a' Mhaim. This peak is almost in the centre of the range, so is one of the best viewpoints of all. Gars-bheinn, the most southerly Cuillin, can be climbed from almost any side. Sgurr Alaisdair by the Great Stone Shoot, and Sgurr nan Gillean by the " tourist route," may also be ascended, but in both the last hundred feet or so involve some rock-climbing, and hands as well as feet are required. For Sgurr nan Gillean the route leaves the Loch Brittle path at the ruins of the cottage, crosses the Allt Dearg Mòr by stepping-stones (often covered after rain) and leads to the left across the moor. It is better to have the route pointed out at Sligachan. The return should be made, in each case, by the same route. In mist, rain or high wind these " easy " routes will become difficult and should then be avoided.

Whether you wish to do the easy climbs already mentioned or be led up the more difficult ones you should purchase the Scottish Mountaineering Club's *Guide to Skye*. It gives full details of all the climbs, and splendid photographs of the difficulties which must be overcome. It also contains a special map of the Black Cuillin, three inches to the mile.

Recently the S.M.C. have issued a new map of the Cuillin Hills (cloth, 2s. 6d.), much bigger than the one contained in the *Guide Book*. On this the so-called easy routes among the mountains are well marked. If you wish to get to know the Cuillin this map will prove invaluable, though you may not find some of the routes so very easy.

Weather.—It is impossible to prophesy. You must be prepared for anything, yet Skye's reputation for wet weather is quite undeserved. There is lots of mist, to be sure, but often when the Cuillin are hidden in mist there is sunshine at sea-level. Last year in June and part of July there was a succession of perfect days, while in August the weather was very unsettled. June is often the best month in Skye. You maun gang and hope for the best! You are a poor tramper if you cannot take to the moor roads joyously on a stormy day, with the smirr of Highland rain in your face and the scent of peat and bog-myrtle in your nostrils. It has been truly said that a journey in Skye is enhanced by the very changeable-ness of the weather. Good weather in Skye is worth waiting for; the rain and the mist will make you appreciate the more those heavenly days which frequently occur.

The tramper who has not been there is bound to ask why so much has been written about the wonderful charm of Skye—an island almost bare of trees and often "bleak wi' rain and black wi' peat." Let him go there and he will query no longer. Words cannot express the kindliness of its people, nor convey the glamour it casts over the visitor.

Go then, walker, to Eilean à Cheo, while you are young and strong of foot. Tramp over its peaty moorlands. Explore its noble corries. Climb its high mountains. And may you have *cloud-white wander-weather*.

APPENDIX

How these place-names do joy impart
To many a homesick Highland heart
That owns afar the potent art
Infused by Celtic ardour.

EVEN a slight knowledge of Gaelic makes a visit to Skye more interesting. The meaning of some of the place-names has already been given. Their study is a fascinating one, commemorating, as they do, ancient myths and legends, battles long forgot, and heroes of the past.

Here are given only the more common nouns and adjectives found in Bartholomew's half-inch-to-the-mile map of Skye.

This map is something of a mixture. Many of the Gaelic names are now given in English; some are given in Gaelic at one place and in English at another. A good number of the place-names are of Norse origin, and others may be a mixture of Gaelic and Norse. Nearly all place-names starting with *H* are Norse or Scandinavian. These mostly occur in Trotternish and Duirinish.

As to pronunciation, better listen to the natives. Where Mhadaidh is pronounced *Vatee*, and Dearg *Jerrag*, you will understand there are certain pitfalls. Do remember that *bh* and *mh* are pronounced like *v* if at beginning of a word and are silent when in the middle of a word; *mh* at end of a word is pronounced as *v*, while *bh* may be silent—*i.e.* bheag = *veg*, ramh = *rav*, Sgurr Dubh na Da Bheinn = *Surr Doo na Da Ven*; *c* at beginning of a word = *k*; *sh* or *th* at beginning of a word = *h*; *fh* at beginning of a word is silent.

The mountains have many different names.

Beinn or ben = mount—generally applied to mountains in Scotland.

Sgurr = a separate mountain, like a beinn but more rocky. All the Cuillin peaks are sgurrs.

Creag = a rock—usually an outlying spur of a mountain.

Meall = a lumpy hill—a good many in Skye—*e.g.* Meall a' Mhaim.

Monadh = a flat-topped hill. MacLeod's Tables are the best example, but these have their Norse names, Healavals. Only a few monadhs in map of Skye.

As an Englishman once said:

" A mountain's a mountain in England, but when
The climber's in Scotland it may be a Beinn,
A Creag or a Meall, a Spidean, a Sgòr,
A Càrn or a Monadh, a Stuc or a Torr."

Similarly, a river may be a river, a burn, an abhuinn, an allt or a lòn:

Abhuinn (pronounced *avin*) = Gaelic of river. The larger ones are given in English, the smaller ones in Gaelic; often named from the strath they flow through, or corrie of origin—*e.g.* Abhuinn Strath na Creithach.

Allt=burn; usually in Gaelic, but sometimes in English; usually named from corrie of origin, or with such adjectives as red, black, big, little, etc.

Lòn=also a burn, but whereas allt is a rushing, tumbling burn, lòn is a slow, muddy burn. Allt comes down over rocks, lòn flows over flat marshy ground.

Adjectives.—There is no neuter in Gaelic, and the adjectives take the gender of the noun they qualify, *h* being inserted into the word to indicate the feminine. This of course changes the pronunciation —*e.g.* mòr (*m.*) as spelt, but mhòr (*f.*)=*vor*. Thus we get: càrn mòr=a big cairn (*m.*); creag mhòr=a big rock (*f.*). Similarly with the others.

Bàn, bhàn=white (pronounced *ban* and *van*).

Beag, bheag=little.

Buidhe, bhuidhe=yellow (pronounced *bui* and *vui*).

Fada, fhada=long.

Fionn, fhionn=fair, beautiful.

Dearg, dheirg=red, pink.

Dubh, dhubh=black.

Garbh, gharbh=rough.

Glas, ghlas=grey.

Ruadh, rhuadh=red.

Nouns.—Nouns and adjectives in genitive case have also an *h* inserted. These are said to be

aspirated, as the sound is softened, or silent—*e.g.*
coire beag = a little corrie; sgurr a' choire bheag
= the peak of the little corrie.

Aird = promontory.

Airidh = shieling. In the olden days the crofters
moved to a shieling in the hills during the
summer. The practice is not followed now, and
most of the summer shielings are ruins. They
are not marked on the map, but names of
many are preserved locally, usually with a
legend attached to them. Their site is remembered in the names of burns and bridges
—*e.g.* Drochaid Airidh na Suiridhe—Bridge of
Shieling of Courtship.

Baca = ridge — *e.g.* Baca Ruadh = Red Ridge
(Trotternish).

Bealach = pass (between two hills)—*e.g.* Bealach na
Sgairde = Pass of Screes (between Glamaig and
Beinn Dearg).

Bruach = brae, steep place—*e.g.* Bruach na Frithe.

Cadha = pass.

Cailleach = an old woman.

Camas = bay—sometimes English, sometimes Gaelic.

Caisteal = castle.

Clach = stone, always in Gaelic—*e.g.* Rudha nan
Clach.

Cladach = shore, beach—*e.g.* Cladach a' Ghlinne
(Strathaird).

Cnoc = knoll—always in Gaelic; occurs frequently.

Coire = corrie, crescent-shaped hollow.

Cuil = nook, recess.

Daraich = oak—*e.g.* Allt Daraich (Sligachan).

Drochaid = bridge.

Druim = ridge—*e.g.* Druim nan Ramh.

Dun = hill, fort.

Dunan = little hill, little fort.

Each = horse.

Eas = waterfall—nearly always in English.

Eoin = bird.

Glac = hollow.

Iolair = eagle.

Leathad = slope—*e.g.* Leathad na Craobh = Slope of Trees (Torran).

Oir = gold

Rathad = road.

Rudha = point — sometimes English, sometimes Gaelic.

Seileach = willow.

Sgeir = skerry, reef near coast—always in Gaelic, with adjectives, black, big, little, etc.

Sithein = fairy, fairy hillock — always in Gaelic, occurs very frequently.

Sron = a nose or point.

Stob = point.

Strath = valley.

Uamh = cave—usually in English, sometimes Gaelic —*e.g.* Uamh Oir = Cave of Gold (Kilmuir).

INDEX

INDEX